THE MIRROR OF A MIND

THE IMAGE OF AIR

SAUL

THE LAST CRUSADE

BY

Algernon Sydney Logan

Collected Edition

NATIONAL PUBLISHING COMPANY
PHILADELPHIA
1934

THE MIRROR OF A MIND

A POEM

"Give me the glass and therein will I read."
KING RICHARD II.

THE MIRROR OF A MIND

CANTO FIRST.

I.

Bright clouds which are the spirits of the skies!
Even now, as ever, while ye soar above,
On you the dying day has fixed his eyes
With a last look of sympathy and love,—
Fired by that gleam which through all time hath
strove
To light the soul from out its darkened isle;—
Ye are so pure, so heavenly, that ye move
Like angels answering back day's fading smile,
Though cold corporeal Earth is bathed in night the
while.

II.

A melancholy splendor lights the peaks
Of the wind-wafted mountains, where they rise,
A jagged chain which the horizon streaks;

Rearing a barrier which our sight defies;
Floating above the Infinite which lies
Beyond the land of tribute to the mind.
This glare of dissolution would disguise
Day's death with lurid lustre, ye we find
Each swift-receding ray grows less and less defined.

III.

Dim misty nothings on the horizon's verge,
With weird significance rise one by one
From the abode of shades; and as they merge
Like living letters range themselves upon
The arras of the world, where now is shown
The "Menè, Menè," of a monarch's might.
The last faint glimmer lingering all alone,
Slips like to water from the grasp of sight—
Lost like the foam in ocean;—Gray rolls on the night!

IV.

With feeble glimmer, through the deepening blue,
The greater stars come slowly one by one;
The lesser follow, though at first but few,
Yet brightening as new numbers still are shown;
Feeding upon the darkness which has grown
Till all around is lost, save objects near;
And these recede till—now I am alone
With the wide heavens, sparkling, flashing, clear—
One world hath faded that a thousand may appear!

V.

Ye stars, eternal children of the night!
Pale with a thousand vigils! envious Time
Hath passed beneath you in his withering flight,
Nor dared the awful infinites to climb
From whence with undimmed eyes and mien sublime,
For ages ye have watched man bowing down
Beneath his load of misery and crime;
Yet drinking with his eyes your radiance thrown,
To break his night of life, nor leave him Sorrow's
    own.

VI.

Guardians and friends of man! whose unseen hands
Grasp the dim chains which check the mad career
Of this our world, which through the glittering bands
Of stars would rush to chaos, till the clear
Light of the sun would fade and disappear
Across the airy desert:—not so now;
For Earth must carry each succeeding year,
Dense with its fruits, and while ye gaze below,
Move on with measured pace, nor ever swift nor slow.

VII.

Your very names are histories, and ye hold
The brightest deeds of the past world on high,
Which else were buried now all still and cold,
Within that grave which doth forever lie,
Waiting the present hour that passes by,

Following Time's steps and drinking in his waste;
Ye have taught man to lisp Eternity.
Oh, wildly flashing stars! the light ye cast
Guides my mind backward, for ye are the endless
    Past!

VIII.

And men do call thee dead, thou mighty Past!
Thou father of our thoughts! whence man derives
All that he knows—Let Time outstrip the blast!
He takes from others, to thee only gives;
Thou art the giant charioteer, who drives
The magic car of the o'erpassing hour,
Born at thy mandate, and which only lives
To be thy food: Immortal changeless Power!
Thou art the light of life, brightest when tempests
    lower.

IX.

From darkness into darkness glides the hour,
Inflicting change, yet changing 'neath the view—
Apparelled from the mind—a magic power—
A ghost to me, a harlequin to you—
A medium whose capricious falseness through
Must come our light—a prism colorless,
Yet shedding on each side a different hue;
Thus is the mind bewildered, nor can guess
Whether grief, joy, be shades, or that which they
    profess.

X.

Joy is the very shadow of a smile,
Sorrow the mere reflection of a frown,—
Yet these themselves are shadows, and beguile
The heart to deem the world without its own.
He who would mine the silver that is thrown
Forever by the moon upon the sea,—
Floating upon a single spot alone,
Yet drifting by your side eternally—
He only from such dreams would forge reality.

XI.

From hoary infancy to hoary age,
From trembling growth to tottering decay,
From the mere blank to the o'erwritten page,
From the green wood to ashes cold and gray,
From things unknown to things long past away,
How small the span, how fleeting is the fire,
How brief the gleam that falls upon our clay,
How short the hour in which the heart's wild lyre
Will vibrate to the winds of change, love, hope, desire.

XII.

Why wander bone-strewed fields to meditate
On human mutability? why rove
O'er sites of cities now depopulate,
To feel how all things toward Destruction move?
Why muse on wormy, mould-filled skulls to prove

How beauty, hope, joy, life, speed fast away?
An eye averted which did beam with love,
A single frown—a smile but yesterday—
More than all empires dead, speak change, decline,
 decay.

XIII.

Towards love's sun doth bliss, that butterfly
Soar on his fragile wing, nor knows the day
Which viewed his birth shall see his bright plumes lie
Dim in the dust; a single snow-flake may
Hurl him forever from his joyous way;
A single breath from out the northern heaven
Will quench with stormy clouds the autumnal ray;
And in an instant he is madly driven
Down on some chilly stream, with pinions wrenched
 and riven.

XIV.

When Exultation bursts upon the soul,
Crushing the barriers reared by years and pride;
When the lip curls—eye flashes; when Control
Reels backward tott'ring, and the long denied
And boastful tongue pours forth what we would hide;
When to thy fellow-man thy heart grows warm,
Grasp thy mind's tiller, trust not to the tide!
Moments of perfect bliss e'er bode us harm—
The gentle sea gull's coming tells the wildest storm.

XV.

The boisterous sound and sweep of my own lyre
Have caught me up and carried me away,
Borne on the breath of an unquenched desire
To slake the thirst for thought, and to allay
Our aspirations for a purer ray
Than that which we inherit: but my song
Bids me return to whence my thoughts did stray—
Years which came singly, but now form one throng—
That atom of the Past which doth to me belong.

XVI.

I gaze into the camera of years,
And there behold a scene of sleepless pain—
Hopes ever walking hand in hand with fears,
Ambition scourging the reluctant brain,
Trying to strengthen it with stripes in vain,
Cursing the boy because not yet the man,
And blighting his best efforts with disdain;
These tortured not by chance, but with a plan,
And dimmed the deep-set spark which they would
    over-fan.

XVII.

But these came later, and still torture now;
My backward glances pass them, wandering
To meet one distant spot where lives a glow;
As when around our pathway shadows cling,
Far as the eye can reach the sunbeams fling

Their lustre o'er some valley green and smooth.
Sweet hour that drinks and tastes not of the spring!
Pure hour that hears and doubts not of the truth!
Fair hour of shapeless bliss, blest time of earliest
    youth!

XVIII.

Joy is the whetstone of the scythe of Time—
How early must our childhood wake to pain!
How soon must we be taught that thought is crime!
And strive with helpless hands, too oft in vain,
To file in secret the oppressive chain,
Which other minds upon our reason throw;
Seeking to prove with eager, nerveless brain,
That what is said need not, for all, be so—
Oh this is agony! behold the dawn of woe!

XIX.

But childhood waned, and as I older grew,
My glance was upward, though I knew not why;
Above me Happiness the martlet flew;
I marked her pathway through the stormy sky,
Enraptured with her pinions' gorgeous dye;
And oft she faded from my straining sight,
Oft in her wavering course swept swiftly nigh—
I knew not she was footless, and her flight
Eternal, and I deemed she might, she could alight!

XX.

Power, Envy, Hatred, sent their shadowy brood—
Words, gestures, looks, the half indifferent air,
Oppression unavowed yet understood,
Assent equivocal, and praise most rare,
The hint that all men all your talents share,
The boundless praise of others your own knoll;
Like phantom birds with brazen beaks, these tear
The stoutest heart, and check the boldest soul,
And with their poisoned wings blot out the distant
    goal.

XXI.

The marbles of the mind around me lie,
Opinions, both my own and others, piled
Confusedly in heaps; from these I try
A stately and consistent dome to build—
A palace of the brain; but feverish, wild,
To work with me my heart I cannot tame,
To fruitless toil it will not be beguiled:—
Thought eats away the mind which has no aim—
A hidden agony, a pain without a name.

XXII.

'Tis night; a youth is from his window leaning;
The moon and stars together slowly rise;
The scene upon his face prints not its meaning,—
The passing clouds, the moonlit, starry skies

He sees not, though, reflected in his eyes;
His ear receives, not hears the vesper chant:
For he has found this truth which few can prize—
That all substantial things for which men pant,
Objects of sense, are air—our thoughts are adamant.

XXIII.

From my own past I gladly turn away;
Our life begins long after birth, and ends
Too often ere we die, and I delay
To seize each coming Present as it tends
To form what I shall be, and ever bends
The bow, and fits the arrow which belong
Unto the morrow. Round me there extends
A world of beauty which demands my song—
Tints, shadows, colors, rays, commingling in one
        throng.

XXIV.

For now sad Autumn with his plaintive flute
Upon the hill-tops mournful ditties plays;
Tears doth he shed which stain his russet suit,
Weeping the waste which yet he never stays,—
Save when at times his march he still delays
And toward the parted summer turns him round,
With melancholy smile and longing gaze;
With red and yellow leaves his head is crowned,
And ever as he walks some rustle to the ground.

XXV.

The time exalts the spirit while it grieves—
Birth and decay in beauty ever vie—
The sunless sunlight of the yellow leaves
Lives everywhere, and mocks the cloudy sky;
Shedding o'er all the world a golden dye—
The light of Desolation; far and near,
As setting suns defy mortality,
On wood, and glen, and hill-side doth appear
This smile amidst despair—bright sunset of the year.

XXVI.

The sunset of the year! behold, the trees
Like evening clouds grow brighter as we gaze!
Lit by an orb we see not; by degrees
Melting into a universal blaze;
Filling the upward eye with wild amaze,
Which views these glories of the closing day—
A shattered and strewed rainbow lines the ways—
Till Autumn's later evening steals their ray,
Leaving them spiritless, unlighted, cold and gray.

XXVII.

Red trees like torches light the Autumn's bier,
Their leaves like sparks fall glowing to the ground;
The golden gleam that earlier did appear
Hath passed away, and sad each sight and sound;

Dead leaves in heaps lie stiffening all around;
Mists rise where'er we gaze with motion slow;
While the faint warble of the distant hound
Lingers upon the air with billowy flow,
Soft, sweet, yet ominous—unfeeling, though so low.

XXVIII.

And as the woodland paths we slowly tread,
A solitary leaf will often stray,
Like to a ghost, from out the piles of dead,
And roll before, as if to point the way
Which we must follow—even to decay;
But glance above, and there behold the buds
Of the next year—these are the unborn May,
Which lives unnoticed in the weeping woods,
And smiles at Winter's might,—his whirlwinds,
    snows and floods!

XXIX.

All that through life we struggle to repress,
All that unites us to the vile and low,
All that would mock the soul and make it less,—
These are Death's spoils—he never aims a blow
At that which most we cherish; but the prow
Sees not the silvery wash that leaves the keel;
The only immortality we know,
We by a kind of phantom memory feel—
Gaze back on days unborn, and past the future steal.

XXX.

There is a faint perception in the mind,
An unsubstantial goad which bids us climb;
Sometimes it seems a wish almost defined,
Again a memory blurred by passing Time,
Anon a half-read prophecy sublime;
And now it lights our living Hope of fame,
Now seems the dim remembrance of a crime,
Which strikes us ere we know from whence it came,
And wakes a heavy throb, half sorrow and half shame.

XXXI.

Dim as the orb that joins the hornèd moon,
Or meteors' trains which vanish in the sky;
Faint as the chimes of distant bells which swoon
Upon the ear, or when they wearily
Toil up against the blast, though flung from nigh,
And scarce may reach us, breathless, feeble, slow;
As ineffective as the sunset's dye
Tinting the chilly foam, or frost on snow,
Or rain upon the ocean, sinking in its flow;

XXXII.

Dim as the phantoms of our future years,
That pass before sad childhood's dreamy eye,
This spirit of the mind, as it appears
Troubling the waters—but why multiply

My images to paint the wind, or try
By ghosts to show a something dimmer still—
So thin that Time, Death, pass it scatheless by—
A might which makes the eye to flash and fill—
The unessential shade, whom Sorrow cannot kill.

XXXIII.

All feel in youth this restlessness within,
This pain which doth our life and aims impeach;
We strive to fight the world in armour thin—
Grasp at a fruit beyond our mortal reach,
Miss it, and say it is not; and then teach
That life is vain, and naught on earth is warm,
Concealing wounds that know nor balm nor leech;
But yet in some this spirit takes a form,
And makes them stem the stream, and battle with
    the storm.

XXXIV.

Life's waves oft whelm our Hope, but ebbing soon,
Behold, it gleams again in flickering lines!
Like the blurred image of the ocean moon
In the wet sands, which tremulously shines,
And with a buried lustre: The heart pines
To flee from those who live chained to the car
Of trifles; but Ambition's blast inclines
To waste at length the soul it bears afar—
The soul, that rising spark, that fain would be a star.

XXXV.

The vastest forms which rise within the soul,
The mightiest children of the laboring mind,
Can never reach Expression's earthly goal;
But wander restless, shadowy, undefined,
Even beneath our gaze to melt inclined:
Like Earth's gigantic, lonely shade are they!
Which even on the moon no rest may find,
But from her breast is rudely torn away,
Left buoyless in space, the Impalpable's dim prey.

XXXVI.

To follow these on leaden wings; to hem
Our world-worn mantle with a cloth of gold;
To graft the ruddy rose upon a stem
Now withering as it stands; or to unfold
The fallen leaf, and from its shape, though cold,
Its fading color and its venous frame,
Recall that beauty sinking fast to mould;
To spur the mind which grows each day more tame—
Behold the noblest life, the loftiest human aim!

XXXVII.

Vain as the Tyrian cloak which the pale cloud
Wraps round his wasting form at even—vain
As castles in the fiery coals, whose proud
Towers dissolve into an ashy rain—

Vain as the memory of a smile when pain
Tortures the writhing lip, this constant war
'Twixt soul and sense, this torture of the brain,
This effort to outstrip the thing we are,
Embodied in a sigh when gazing on a star.

XXXVIII.

Yet pity him who hath no war within—
'Tis vain to call our sleep philosophy!
The elemental jar, the noiseless din,
This is the true, the only alchemy;
Which from the base alloys that men may see
Spread far and near fuses the virgin gold:
Yet oft the strain will shatter suddenly
The crucible which would this fusion hold;
And thus the o'er-labored mind breaks long ere it
        be old.

XXXIX.

I fain would be my soul, which I am not—
Which no man is—and yet which all should be;
But still 'tis comfort in our mortal lot,
To set our soul before us, and to see
Its beauties shine in wild sublimity;
Till admiration deepens into love,
And love becomes absorption, and we flee
Far from the trifling crowd, to dwell above,
Though still our living shade 'mongst soulless men
        may move.

XL.

And if my spirit to this impulse yields;
'Tis humbly, not elated, nor confused;
For I gazed long upon the snowy fields
Which I must tread, before my feet were loosed
From out their native valley; and I mused
On icy winds, or e'er I sought to climb:
The penalty of pain is not refused—
He would leave the sunny vale of time,
Takes for warm human joys the coldly fair Sub-
lime.

XLI.

I write that they who follow me may say,
Not, "this he *wrote*," but "this indeed he *was*."
"This is the life his soul lived day by day."
Men's best thoughts come unmarshalled, without
class;
And I but ope the door for mine to pass
From my own mind into the open air.
To my own being I but hold a glass,
Which shows each changing look, or dark, or fair—
This Mirror paints the new, yet holds the old still
there.

XLII.

Noteless I sing—What life was ever planned?
What thought e'er sent a herald far before?
Who would hold water in an iron band?

In one straight line do streamlets ever pour
From their slight spring down to the ocean's shore?
Why from a thousand flowers round me massed
In wildest beauty choose but three or four?
Or from the marble features of the Past
Hand to posterity a rigid death-like cast?

XLIII.

Scenes with their thoughts, thoughts with their van-
    ished scenes—
All that within me has been most concealed
From blight and mildew—all that living means—
What to my real self has most appealed,—
These I would garner here into one yield,
The humble harvest of my human clay;
But Time before us mows in our own field,
And what Time cuts, Oblivion stacks away,
Reaping what men have sown and tended night and
    day.

XLIV.

My heart is throbbing with a great design—
To catch the spirit of a journeying mind,
And that my own; that where I hope or pine,
Struggle, enjoy, or fondly gaze behind,
Another, following, too, may pause and find
Fresh food for feeling: here I seek to show
Sculptures of thoughts and feelings ne'er defined;
Such hopes, like moonlight sparkles upon snow,
Flash with a light from heaven, yet still remain
    below.

XLV.

Yet shall the spirit cease to seek for fame,
When flame shall point to earth instead of heaven.
Joys shall bedeck a life without an aim
When on the restless clouds by whirlwinds driven,
Eternal flowers bloom: yet there are given
No words to paint that which the soul still strives
To seize and render palpable; but even
He who in his own being deeply dives,
Oft finds no beauty there—yet still believes it lives.

XLVI.

Pure Presence! that dost have thy daily haunt
Within the glitt'ring fleecy Alpine snow;
Whose radiant smile comes floating down aslant
From out the Autumn sunset's hazy glow;
Thou spirit of ideal beauty! slow
To penetrate the heart—why hast thou made
No fixed abode in mortal bosom, though
Thy form is ever seen by rock and glade?
Thou art the ghost of Joy, that flittest but to fade.

XLVII.

The night walks forth, and through the mists of
        heaven
Swings her dim lantern which we call the moon;
While racing clouds around the link are driven,
Through the white masses swift she makes it scoon;

But holds it motionless to gaze, as soon
As the dank vapors pass: the air is chill,
The cricket chirps, then sinks into a swoon—
Perchance his last; the cedars dark and still,
Untiring sentinels! seem outposts on the hill.

XLVIII.

The white frost gleams around, the phantom snow,
Which lives but as the breath when blown on glass—
Cold child of morning, dying in the glow
Of the high sun! for often as ye pass,
Ye see him cowering low where the crisp'd grass—
Is shadowed by some object—all is gone
That marked him for a king—his realm which was
The world, is shrunk into this spot alone—
Until the sun creeps round,—and the pale sprite is
    flown.

XLIX.

The thin-armed and long-fingered naked trees,
Like weird anatomies start on the sight;
They come, we know not whence, by twos and threes,
And seem the magic of a single night.
Why do they strip 'gainst Winter's icy might,
The cloaks they wore when June was all too warm?
They do but doff their mantles for the fight!
Like ships they furl their sails before the storm,
Which whistles madly by, but cannot do them harm.

L.

The dreamy days of silence and of haze,
Making death dear to the enraptured mind,
Have passed away, and now where'er we gaze
The distances are rigid and defined;
Wind-spouts, like water-spouts, become entwined
With the thick dust, and bear it to the sky;
November doth the maniac winds unbind,
Who with transparent fingers twirl on high
The bare, bleak, rugged limbs,—so white, so cold,
    so dry.

LI.

Times are there when the senses fail and sink,
And when Thought's walls around contracting seem
Till our world narrows to a cell; we shrink
Into our altered selves; we know we dream,
And strive to wake, yet cannot; not one gleam
Of light our present, past, and future hold;
All life seems vain, our toil we folly deem,
Forgetting we *have* felt, and are not old—
Then rise within the mind these longings manifold:

LII.

Something to feel before the heart grows hard;
Something to think with which no doubting strives;
Something to sing ne'er sung by mortal bard;
Something to see which perfect fulness gives,
And wakes no longing which the spirit rives,—
As do the ocean, star, cloud, sunset, bird;
Something to love incarnate, which yet lives
All undefiled by touch, or thought, or word—
Mind cannot all suffice, still Nature *will* be heard.

CANTO SECOND.

I.

Within the drooping vine the wind doth linger,
Straying across its mystic warp and woof;
The rain keeps tapping with his fairy finger,
In sad monotony upon the roof;
While the faint plash of a retreating hoof
Flings back upon the ear its wat'ry sound.
I gaze into the gloom from all aloof,
Save the all-potent nothings spread around—
Silence and night, mere voids, which yet wake
    thoughts profound.

II.

Silence, who hath not felt thy thrilling power,
When having spoken with a cheerful air
To one we deemed near by at twilight's hour,
We found that thou alone wert waiting there!
Or listening for dead feet upon the stair—
E'en though we know them buried, and the wreath
Our hands have hung—'tis thine to wake despair;
Life fears thee, for thy true home is beneath—
All know thee for the mate, companion, friend of
    Death.

III.

Night, thou art Death! inwoven with his might;
Darkness doth ever sit in dying eyes;
Lo! the dead planets are bereft of light—
Their bloodless corpses stiffen in the skies—
Rivers their veins, deep seas their arteries,
Solid and still; there doth thy presence keep
Death incorruptible: thy gentlest guise
Folds us in tender arms, and soothes our sleep—
Then softly beckons Death upon our souls to creep.

IV.

But to the waking, velvet-footed Night
Raises the veil which wraps all things by day,
Save those which brush against us, and a light
Streams o'er the Past,—and truth is in its ray!
A moment gone is full as far away
As ages past—Time is a whole—years be
But suppositions framed for human clay;
Like lines of latitude upon the sea,
All helpless to divide the waters rolling free.

V.

We move between two mighty doors of glass,
Future before us, clearer Past behind;
We pine, we long these narrow bounds to pass,
Which though transparent all our movements bind;

The view before most pains the gazing mind,
For that strange sadness which doth overspread
The world, we chiefly in the future find—
Sighs breathed forth o'er a Future which is dead,
Outweigh the fleeting tears which for the Past are
    shed.

VI.

To know the flood is still itself the ebb;
To see in the scarce budding rose decay;
To feel that yarn is lacking for the web
Of our ideal life; to view the ray
Fade from *one* face while unborn shadows gray
There fall; to meet an unembodied woe;
To see our soul o'er-mired in our clay—
Such is the Future! felt by us e'en now,
As the pale victim feels the yet ungiven blow.

VII.

The waters of the shadowy fount of Time
Flow silently and softly glide away;
A sphynx's head it is which none may climb,
Darkness within which never felt a ray;
We only see the tingeless current play,
Nor e'er may know how much remaineth there.
Whole civilizations of man's monstrous day
Are but the hours; whose clock upon the air
Flings forth its clangless strokes, which all to count
    despair.

VIII.

Its motion is so slow, and our slight time
Of watching is so short, we cannot see
The fated hand the enormous dial climb
And point the hour; and thus men differently
Compute the point man stands on—none agree;
Some see him young, some bowed with sinking age;
And while they fight the hand moves constantly;
Each calls as witness History's yellow page,
Which cheats philosophy, and mocks the groping
    sage.

IX.

The hour is late, yet ere I take my rest
Let us look forth upon the earth and sky;
The cold rain ceases—flowers it once had blessed—
It wets their bier, yet mocked their agony;
Great furling clouds on unseen masts go by;
A rainbow which the wayward moon hath wrought,
Like to a spirit's smile gleams forth on high—
Ghost of a ghost, translucent aëronaut,
Beauty more beautiful, an unimprisoned thought!

X.

Deep the clear azure of the midnight sky,
Dark even to blackness, fathomless and blind
As seas that never heard the leadsman's cry;
The full meridian moon the trees behind,

Ringless and rayless, white, cold, hard, defined,
Blanches the meadows glistening bleak and bare,
Like fields of snow; a thin ethereal wind
Hastens the moon-lit clouds, so ghostly fair—
White, glittering, pinnacled, the icebergs of the air!

XI.

There is a spot where oft my steps are bent,
Where giant rocks to press the earth are seen
With the deep, heavy, lost abandonment
Of an eternal slumber; and they lean,
And seem as nodding o'er the flickering sheen
Of a slight rill, which hastens on below
'Twixt mossy stones; while many an evergreen
Stretches his muffled arms with movements slow,
As if to stay the stream, and hush its boisterous flow.

XII.

Stern hemlocks up the dark and craggy steep
Stand balanced on the rocks, and feeding seem
Upon the solid stone; while slowly creep
Pale sunbeams through their tops, and softly dream
Far o'er the polished laurel leaves, and gleam
Like moonlight on the waters. Seasons pass,
And leave no foot-prints on the rocks and stream
In this self-centered vale; a mind it has
Which takes no colors from the world's surrounding
    mass.

XIII.

When in her em'rald cloak fair Spring appears,
Kindling a world to love with soft young eyes,
All timidly this spot alone she nears—
The firs and laurels changing not their dyes,
Wave back a wintry answer; Autumn flies,
Shouting of changes—still are they unmoved;
The ice sprite wanders by the stream, and tries
To bridge the waters, and, though vain 'tis proved,
Plants piers along the banks fantastically grooved.

XIV.

Here thoughts ideal, free, untinted, clear,
Live ever in the shade, and ere my feet
Have reached the glen, my steps they seem to hear,
And from the green in shadowy guise to greet
My coming to this wild and feared retreat;
For some do say a sprite of darksome mood
Doth haunt the spot, whom many dread to meet,—
Yet spirit there is none within the wood,
Save the poor tortured shade, the ghost of Solitude.

XV.

Eleven thousand years must slowly pass,
And a new star illumes the northern pole!
And shall not Nature then be as she was
Ere man began her glories to control?
Where then the toil-worn artificial whole,
Commerce and trade, stilts of man's petty pride?

Rivers 'twixt grassy banks may nobly roll,
Where smoky cities now their meadows hide,
And trout leap in the streams by factories deeply
    dyed.

XVI.

Primeval forests lurk beneath the plough,
To rise once more at Solitude's command,
Pushed back, not conquered, as when strong winds
    blow
With transient force the tides from off the land,—
Soon to return and sweep across the sand,
With greater violence the more delayed:
Silence and Loneliness are still at hand,
Though vain our search by stream, and hill, and
    glade;
We deem them ever found, when lo! 'tis but their
    shade.

XVII.

I would not sing man's downfall, for the sake
Of Feeling's glorious sun, whose disc immense,
Broke to a million fragments, still must make
In man's divided bosom dark and dense,
Its scattered home—collectless, unintense:
Yet shall these close extremes ne'er cease to be,
Things of pure intellect and things of sense,
Whose mien would make you deem they easily
Could wear Orion's belt, or toast you with the sea?

XVIII.

Beholding man, as man around we see,
We wonder Death will touch so mean a thing—
That they who never saw reality,
Who o'er pure Nature tawdry drapings fling,
Shall e'er behold the universal king,
The sole controller of life's hidden fire,—
From the cupped flowers, the dimples of the Spring,
To systems whom no weight of time can tire,
Who yet beneath his frown pale, sicken, faint, expire.

XIX.

Yet wonder not, for they are trodden down
Like eyeless worms, that see not the quick stamp
Which makes them earth again: Behold the town!
This populous waste, these airy nothings' lamp—
Here flit the worldlings who the spirit damp,
Their flesh bedizened but their soul in rags!
With voices unimpelled by mind they cramp
Too timid nature—these unsightly snags
Stick on life's boiling stream, and curse it that it
    lags!

XX.

Who gazes through a single skylight pane
Deems all heaven darkened by the smallest cloud;
So they that bend beneath the world's cold chain,
Crushed to the damp mould by their unseen load,

Know of no sun save the faint ray bestowed
Through their dim, distant loop hole—nay; arise!
Rend ye your bonds, the universe endowed
With flower-decked earth and star-emblazoned skies,
Were for one free-born soul too small a Paradise!

XXI.

Perspective rules the country of the mind,
Even as the outer world which meets the eye,
Far mountains there look low and undefined,
Though their gigantic summits pierce the sky;
And heaps of sand, so that they be but nigh,
Poor handfuls at the mercy of all winds,
Blot out the landscape, and seem far more high;
And thus mere nearness ever cheats and blinds
Him who doth gaze on life, and naught but trifles
        finds.

XXII.

Yet there are minds which like to Alpine lakes,
Reflect far-distant mountains; for though they
Must image back the green leaves of the brakes
Which line the margin; though a shadow stray
Across their mirror; though the light oar's spray,
Or darting fish, or swallow's wing, or stone
Thrown by an idler their smooth surface fray,
Still far below those awful snows are shown,
Which though they pass the clouds, the lake beholds
        alone.

XXIII.

As many weathers as the tombstone feels,
Missing no change, day, evening, night, or dawn,
So many impulses the mind conceals;
The youngest motive hath the greatest brawn;
One influence a thousand more will spawn,
And all pull different ways, till hearts grow cold;
Their strength still lasting till our own is gone:—
How can the world so many feelings hold?
Who can resist them best?   The timid, not the bold.

XXIV.

The timid! they who dread their human clay—
Who when the world's vast allied armies come,
To burn their fertile fields, their souls to slay,
Retreat, present no front, and save their home;
All others trust to a redoubt of foam:
The timid! they who guard their inward eye,
Lest it by accident a moment roam
From where 'tis fixed upon their star on high—
These slowly, humbly plod the pathway to the sky.

XXV.

The genie of the lamp which burns within
Will never leave unanswered him who calls;
But first bar out the world's unmeaning din,
And in the starry and gem-lighted halls
Of thy own mind,—in silence which appalls,

Yet wakes thy better being,—there alone,—
While from thy eye a tear of rapture falls,
And thy loose locks by midnight winds are blown,
Rub thou thy talisman, and call its spirits down.

XXVI.

And when the genie comes, as come he will,
Ask for far sight most distant Truth to see,
Sitting upon her adamantine hill,
Cloud-wrapped, unworshipped, voiceless; wearily
Swaying a realmless sceptre, though she be
True queen of earth, source of all beauty there:—
Ask for a heart that will not ever flee
From feelings' touch, and slowly melt in air;
Such first would cheat mankind, at last bring dull
    despair.

XXVII.

The lowliest flower still drinks the evening dew;
Upon the smallest twig the wind will play;
The faintest star-beam falls as far and true
As the sun's glories in the glare of day;
The lightest seed that on the blast can stray,
Within its tiny breast a might doth wield,—
A future lies entranced within its clay;
The dullest eye hath light, though ne'er revealed—
The humblest heart a chord, how deep so e'er con-
    cealed.

XXVIII.

But like a flute washed on a desert shore—
A harp Æolian buried 'neath the mould—
A giftless shrine with a cemented door—
The coin of an age now still and cold,
Which none can value—or a story told
To woods and streams, which lives upon the air,—
But scattered, melted, lost—an echo rolled
Far in the mountain, and still resting there—
Like each, like all the heart, it answers not to prayer!

XXIX.

For other hearts like mountains round us rise,
Seemingly fitted to return all sound—
We shout, but wake no echoes; or we prize
One being, deeming we at length have found
A mirror of ourselves,—our wish is crowned!
We smile into the glass, and start to find,
When we have smiled our image darkly frowned:
How hard at last the struggle to unwind
Dead hopes, which like dead vines, Life's tree so
    closely bind.

XXX.

Men seek to draw from man, e'en though they know
Themselves insolvent, helpless to return;
Seeds of the heart in others we would sow,
Hoping for harvest, while the whirlwinds spurn

Those cast on our own bosoms; still we turn
On things which are not, yet should be our whole,
Eyes dull, or which with other lustre burn:
There is a shining vapor in the soul,
Which could it be condensed, no more to heaven
    would roll.

XXXI.

Dark ocean's tides that chisel her bleak cliffs
To sculptured forms of wild sublimity,
Are ruffled, yet unaltered by the skiffs,
Which play upon their bosom; thus the high
Surges which mould our nature still pass by
The lovely forms upon their surface rife,
Which to our deeper being e'er are nigh.
There are no anchors in the barks of life,
Or each fond breast would be a bay to end our
    strife.

XXXII.

Winter, the aged huntsman, now appears,
One who with time hath strengthened, not declined;
His withered cheek the tint of vigor wears;
He seeks for spoil with hard and bitter mind;
With barking winds before him and behind,
Which beat each copse and thicket with keen breath—
They bite at all things in their fury blind,
And chase the clouds the chilly sky beneath—
All that is left exposed they doom to speedy death.

XXXIII.

Winds have found voices, but the streams are dumb,
Nor can they stir the snow-bird's thirst to slake;
The days have shrunk into themselves, all numb
And shivering in their sleep—the nights awake!
The long transparent winter nights, which make
The empire of the moon; and blazoning these
The winter stars upon our vision break—
Sirius, Procyon, Rigel, Betelguese,
Capella, Fomalhaut, flash through the glistening
    trees.

XXXIV.

I loved in childhood, and still love to climb
Most dizzy rocks, and air-surrounded towers,
Where, as it were, beyond the reach of Time,
We lose a moment the dull weight of hours;
Hills, streams, clouds, zephyrs reassert their powers;
The soul bursts forth, as breaks the narrow span
Of daily view, and distance dim devours;
Our angel smiles as we the horizon scan,
And feel the world contains more Nature still than
    Man.

XXXV.

I love to sit and watch the setting sun
Slow sinking down athwart the western wave,
Ere yet the purple twilight hath begun
To strew his violets o'er the dead day's grave;

While at my feet the rocks the ripples lave,
Flinging their jets aloft in sparkling showers;
And glowing sails like stars the ocean pave;
And memories long forgot of youthful hours,
Make life's o'ertrodden path not wholly void of
 flowers.

XXXVI.

But when the orb sinks nearer to the sea,
The sunlit sails do one by one expire,
Like stars at morn; and gazing drearily,
We feel that wildering heart-ache, that desire
To gain the ideal realm to which aspire
Our weary thoughts; now from the gathering gloom
Stalks Retrospect in sad and gray attire—
Life's early flowers are gone, and in their room
Behold long willow streamers waving o'er a tomb!

XXXVII.

Oh, Memory! oh, Memory! away!
With all thy thousand forms and colorings;
Pale evening star of our declining day!
Thine is the unseen hand that ever flings
A mantle o'er the coffined Past, and wrings
Dew from life's granite, and from seas of woe,
Sounding their depths, a few slight pearlets strings:
These are thy deeds, thy shapes,—but what art thou?
Art thou impalpable? I would thy essence know.

XXXVIII.

Ay, ether's self indeed! but stern of mood;
Thou art the spectre painter of the soul—
Thy darkest pictures in strong light are stood,
The fair in shadow; and to us the whole
Forms a sad gallery, for the eyes will roll
To fix on sketches which all beauties spoil;
And thus men strive these glances to control,
Lest following eyes see all and mock their toil,
Forgetting other's sight the shifting lights must foil.

XXXIX.

I've loved to gaze upon the Alps, where sweeping,
The winds their glittering grain forever sow;
A thousand winters past there still are sleeping
Upon each other's breasts in tiers of snow.
My heart warmed to those summits, like the glow
Which kissed their pale cold cheeks at close of day;
Something in things thus still which gaze below,
Strangers to motion which is but decay,
Speaks to what in ourselves would live beyond our
    clay.

XL.

A moment wait, ye thoughts in eager crowds!
The eternal rose which blooms but in the sky,
Whose scattered petals are the ruddy clouds,
Sheds o'er the world a universal dye,
Surpassing speech; all earth is heaven, and vie

Hills, streams, trees, grasses, snow, each peeping
 stone,
With the immortal; Man's heart is his eye!
What winter's eve was e'er so fair?—'tis gone—
Save the faint feeble gleam which in this page is
 shown.

XLI.

Oh! that some cunning workman of the mind,
Could frame a magic, viewless door, which they
Who seek the paths of thought might close behind,
And bar return: like feudal vassals gay
Our better thoughts rush on; but one delay
Makes fewer helms and halberds round us gleam,
And the bright host doth softly melt away,
Till gazing round alone we inly deem
There were no fields to win,—'twas but a troubling
 dream.

XLII.

The prattle of our children,—the hoarse hum
Of thousand voices pitched in tones of trade,—
Men hurrying to and fro,—the cries that come
From factions,—and book-whisperings that persuade
Glory a myth, and all our thoughts degrade,
Till genius' self seems cold, and life grows tame,—
That bustle which to live must still be made,—
Shut from our ears the enchanted flute of Fame,
Which though it be unheard, still warbles on the
 same.

XLIII.

Few find on earth the boon which they would seek,
Yet know they drink from a polluted spring;
A blush in secret burns the brazen cheek;
They feel that something to which poets sing,
Which fain would soar, but in them hath no wing,
To mount that ether which the bravest awes;
And years thus pass unheeded, and yet bring
New pains for which they dread to know the cause,
But wear a sculptured smile, and for spears brandish
    straws.

XLIV.

Within youth's grasp man's noblest aims are laid,
But middle age beholds them far, nor pines;
Till noon through seas of golden beams we wade,
Which climb the mountains as our sun declines;
Until this spirit-lustre only shines
Upon the ever varying clouds, which skim
Far, far above; reflected memory twines
Fantastic wreaths on our horizon's rim—
We gaze, and gaze, until all earth and heaven grow
    dim.

XLV.

Hues of the even, sombre yet serene!
Shades from the coming night thrown o'er the soul!
Shadows, which foil the hands that fain would glean
From our reaped fields but one more straw of toll!

Dim forms, who can behold ye, and control
One cry for Time to check his mad career,
Prizing too late the oft neglected goal?
Who loves the coming as the parting year?
We curse our endless toil, yet pine when rest is near.

XLVI.

Our hours are post-boys, who throughout the day
Have loitered listlessly against our will;
But as they near their goal, and shadows gray
Gather around, dash onward through the chill:
Or should I say that hopes and loves are still
The foaming steeds which drag our lagging wain
To the bright top of life's most stubborn hill?
But there they are unharnessed all by Pain—
The car runs down alone, and ever speed doth gain.

XLVII.

Smiles, angels of the lip, are seen no more;
The vestal of the eyes hath fled away.
Where are the souls that seemed to live before
In every leaf, each cloud, each heavenly ray?
Leaves stir, clouds float, as brightly dawns the day,
As fair on sleeping waters sleeps the star—
The children of the heart, oh! where are they?
Where dreams at noonday dwell, a country far,
Where sage and sober thoughts at wild weird mid-
    night are.

XLVIII.

Stillness condensed and gathered into form!
Behold it there! the pallid corpse-like snow—
Who can believe it came upon the storm,
Or e'er had motion, as it sleeps there now,
A spirit-marble covering all below?
And yet the sprite upon the whirlwind climbs,
And while the crowded clouds in masses go,
Flings great white serpents o'er their ragged brims,
Which lie all motionless along the crooked limbs.

XLIX.

A winter's eve: there is no cloud to dim
The horizon's feeble pink, so coldly clear,—
A great blue goblet with a rosy rim,
Turned downward o'er the earth, the skies appear;
Dead weeds and grasses, withered, brown and sere,
Lift o'er the snow their seedless tufts and limbs;
No living sound invades the silence drear;
The wind with printless feet the snow-drift skims,
Wrapped in his viewless cloak, singing his pilgrim
    hymns.

L.

The night is clear and moonless; the stars gleam
Peopling the void.—Oh, dwellers of the sky!
Lost in your own existence do ye seem,
For ye *are* rapture! and your forms on high

Shine with an inborn splendor; silently
Looking a sacred language from afar,
Whose words are feelings; vainly man would try
To grasp their fullest meaning—boundless are
Our senses and our thoughts,—beyond them glows
    the star!

LI.

There is a silence in the ocean's roar,
A hush within the moaning of the wind,
And in the crash of cataracts which pour
From mountain heights, a quiet to the mind—
A thunder with the stillness is combined
Which wraps the stars! With day that nature dies
Which makes man mortal; starlight is entwined
With our soul's life—our awe-struck soul, that tries
To drink serenity, whose fount is in the skies.

LII.

The snow is nested high in the forked limbs,
And there alights the dawn's first feeble ray;
The eastern line a second evening climbs;
White swan-like clouds that westward wing their
    way,
In serried flocks towards the close of day.
Now eastward slowly move, and on their wings
Some golden glances glitter: Morning gray,
O'er stiffened meads, and bristling trees, and springs
All voiceless, hard and dry, his pallid lustre flings.

LIII.

But wintry objects check my outward eye;
The aggressive cold doth seem to drive within
All thoughts, as men shrink back instinctively
From those more self-wrapt than themselves, and in
Reserve their masters: but all those who win
No bays to-day, think straightway how before
They gained a crown—thus memories now begin
To rise.—Hark! for my mind hath heard a roar—
Once more, oh, ocean! do I stand upon thy shore.

LIV.

Like hair plucked by thy wild remorseless hands
From the dread things in thy dread custody,
The fibrous sea-weed strews the yielding sands;
Like great, white, frightened birds which seek to fly,
And spread their snowy pinions toward the sky,—
Then settle down again,—the phœnix foam
Flies up along the coast; whose girdle high
Around thy giant limbs doth circling come—
Own, 'tis a rope of sand which checks thy will to
    roam!

LV.

Oh, Sea, the waves thy cymbals ever beat,
With ceaseless clang, monotonously slow,
Melodious measures which eternal feet
Alone could follow; while the billows flow,

The winds across them wander, and oft blow
Their fifes and trumpets; but as slowly sink
The evening shades, thy features sharper grow,
And wear a deadly look from which all shrink—
Wild voices seem to talk, laugh, whisper round thy
    brink.

LVI.

We go, return, depart, return again,
But Thought still sits beside the sounding shore,
Far from the haunts of hollow-minded men;
Infinity's wild voice is ocean's roar!
Hark to the billows' shout as on they pour!
Each hath a tongue that speaks in accents clear
The secret of the world, the unwritten lore;
All that we know of life waves image here,—
They ebb but to return, break but to reappear.

LVII.

And thus new waves of life forever rolling,
Forever break upon death's ice-bound coast;
Each waving hare-bell its own knell is tolling,
Yet not a leaf or petal e'er is lost:
The fairest flowers felled by early frost,
The noblest soul cut down before its prime,
But fade away that a more lovely host
Forth from their ashes into life may climb,
The same with full-blown strength, in beauty more
    sublime.

LVIII.

The breath which filled my humble reed is spent—
The night is come in which no man may work—
The staff is broke on which my spirit leant—
The thoughts which in my inmost being lurk
Are speechless: From the all-surrounding murk
Two forms alone arise, Fate and Decay;
The last I know full well and would not shirk,—
The other's face is sternly turned away,
To quench my mind with doubt, and quell me with
    dismay.

LIX.

What I have felt shall others ever feel?
What I have sown with toil shall I e'er reap?
Shall my voice ring afar with echoing peal,
Or shall I be as those who in their sleep
Deem they have cried aloud, while their lips keep
Unbroken stillness? 'Twere in vain to try
To wring from out the inexorable deep
Aught that the yearning mind may satisfy—
Yet refuge still remains to fix the wandering eye.

LX.

The true tragedian for one only plays,
One eager face which he beholds below.
Upturned to his with an enraptured gaze,
Seizing his very thoughts ere words may flow,

And gaining on his utterance; even so,
If from earth's millions one ear drink my strain,
If in one heart I may awake a glow,
Or for one bosom win surcease of pain,
Let Darkness dye his frown! my toil is not in vain.

LXI.

Perchance this lay I shall once more resume;
The future thoughts that now I cannot see,
Which stand arrayed between me and the tomb,
May seek to live in music; tremblingly
I still would hope that I may yet, more free,
With higher heart, less soulless scenes among,
Play as I journey onward—it may be—
I know not—But my thoughts have found a tongue!
Though soon my soul grow old, still here 'tis ever
    young.

LXII.

But still I feel a shrinking and a doubt—
Long have I striven—ah! perhaps in vain;
My Hope sinks low, a breath might blow it out;
More frequent grow despondency and pain;
My soul seems launched upon a shoreless main:—
What rose unwatered still blooms on the same?
What captive sinks not 'neath a life-long chain?
What lamp unfed can yet preserve its flame?
What heart still float aloft without the breath of
    Fame?

LXIII.

We live in gloomy days, 'neath sombre skies,
Which pour down ever sleet, and snow, and hail;
And vapors dark and dank around us rise,
Breeding dull slugs and cold worms, that assail
The flowers which strive with loveliness to veil
The bare, black, lifeless mould of earth in vain;
But should these loathely things of slime prevail,
To blight the ambitious nurslings of my brain,—
Still there are springs of joy which man can never
    stain.

LXIV.

A spider's web with starlight dew besprinkled—
A wave which the uprising moon hath lit—
An autumn leaf ere time his cheek hath wrinkled—
The unbought smiles of infancy that flit
Unquestioned by—a few bright pages writ
By slumbering hands—such straws to planks may
    grow,
Clutched by the grasping mind, sustaining it
To stem the waters of disgust and woe,
Which rise with battling tides, to whelm us in their
    flow.

LXV.

The sparkles of the ocean as they fall—
Translucent tongues that dwell within the winds—
The voices of the locust hours that crawl,
With blast athwart the gardens of men's minds—

The slow drag of the anchor that ill binds
Forever drifting Change—the strange impress
Of past on present, and the voice that finds
Its way from out the void,—their mysteries
Infuse into my soul, and bid her mock distress.

LXVI.

I feel as I had reached the ocean's shore,
And found all silence there! the jostling band
Of my own thoughts has hastened on before,
And left me here alone; my song doth stand
And beckon to its echo, which had planned
A swift and loud return; but now is blown
Into the Future's still-retreating land;
Where it may ever wander up and down,
Nor e'er return till I can catch no earthly tone.

THE IMAGE OF AIR

AND OTHER POEMS

CONTENTS

THE IMAGE OF AIR.

It was the early Autumn, and the wind,
Like some lone maiden half to sport inclined,
And half to sadness, who through woodland ways
Moves aimless, singing wild and broken lays,
Sang restlessly amidst the restful tombs.
Now soft it breathed upon the hanging blooms
Of salvia, which with conquest-loving hue
Around the base of many a statue grew,
Making their icy pallor more complete;
And now with hollow laugh for madness meet,
Discordant laugh of Destiny, the wind,
Like one too heartless e'en to be unkind,
Seized on the leaves by Summer's passion seared,
And bore them from the present.
                                    As I neared
The centre of the spot the evening fell—
Pale Evening, with her mind-completing spell,
Whose gentle hand, invisible, is prone
To bear the balance of our musings down,
Giving due weight to thoughts impalpable,
By day too little reckoned. Evening fell.
The unstable gilding of the western sky,
A moment hence too brilliant for the eye,
Began to slowly tarnish and to fade;
Around me gleamed from dusky copse and glade—
Some straight and tall, some leaning to decay—

The emblems pale of effort past away.
The youthful tombs were white as drifted snow,
The aged dark—they darker ever grow—
Forming grim contrast to man's destiny,
Who still grows whiter as the years creep by.
My thoughts went wandering 'midst the mindful
    stones,
Mindful of names of long-forgotten bones,
Culling some mosses from mortality.—
Thoughts are there which do cheat the mental eye,
So complex is their nature: now they seem
Near and familiar, now a sudden gleam
Will lightning-like show cloud-forms far away;
Now do they move as reasonings cold and gray,
Now as warm memories passionate sweep along;
Now as one shape, now as a spirit throng
Such musings meet us, till their sense to hold
We fain must press them to one stable mould—
We consciously with form our thoughts endow
That we may treat with them. With motion slow
From out the vapors of the coming night
A shadow rose before me—no grim sprite,
The child of superstition—but a shade
By me from thoughts of saddest import made.
Aged he seemed, though not yet near his prime—
A withered flower bids us think of time,
E'en though the wrinkles on its velvet cheek
Were furrowed by the hour; his mien was bleak—
As if 'midst magic mountains lingering,
He deep had drunk of some enchanted spring
Within whose every bubble lurked a year;
With careless steps unmeasured he drew near—
Then sudden paused—but even his very pause

Was, like his motions, restless, and the laws
Which ruled his looks and motions were unknown,
For these were rhythmless and each alone—
As the long tendrils of neglected vines
O'er casements hanging in entangled lines,
Sway without concert to the wind's wild strain,
And tap with aimless fingers on the pane.
Oh, he was beautiful beyond compare,
His face than man's, nay, more than woman's fair,
Yet 'twas a beauty that with pained amaze
Filled the beholder; for beneath the gaze
It seemed to fade, yet gazing none might know
If it had faded, or was always so.
Through all his being, even to his sigh,
There breathed a palpable uncertainty.
To look upon him was to feel a pang,
A dread, though none might say from whence it
          sprang—
A straining of the mind, bewilderment,
Hope and suspense in strange confusion blent.
The wildest voices of the mind awoke
Within his presence, and as forth they broke
Into a hurried chant, pale Memory
Holding her solemn harp stood silent by,
And struck wild chords between the wilder staves—
A sound of question, restless as the waves!
For at his sight there swept across the soul
A consciousness of thoughts beyond control,
As from the past when feverishly we strive
Some joy forgotten vainly to revive,
Some dream of beauty deaf to Memory's call,
Which once familiar mocks our efforts all.
In all his motions, gestures, features, mien,

An incomplete perfection there was seen,
A loveliness unearthly, wild and free,
From its fair sequence severed. Near to me
The figure drew, then quickly paused again,
As if the creature of his laboring brain;
His eye, which like a wind-tormented flame,
Now pale and blue, now gleaming bright became,
Fell on a fragile tablet which he bore—
His hand flew fast, his thoughts his hand before—
He wrote o'er half the tablet, and anon
Gazed quickly round, as if in quest of one
To whom it might be shown—but none appeared—
Then faded grew his eye, his features bleared:
Dim grew his form, fantastical and gray,
Even as the spirits of the storms when they
Around the moon their magic misty ring
Form hand in hand, and to her footsteps cling.
To stay the shadow ere it grew inwrought
With other forms around, I said, or thought,
"Who art thou that in such phantasmal guise
Still bearest the weight of human energies?"
As memories of dreams to present care,
As crescent moonlight is to midday's glare,
So to all human voices, when he spoke,
The sound I felt, which silence never broke:—
"I am the shape of one who lived in vain,
If being be to be not, since I gain
An entity in speech which is not mine;
Yet mayest thou in this evanescent line
The wraith in words of that which was behold,
As I in form." Ere ceased his utterance cold,
Which seemed remembered and not heard, he gained
A marble shaft, and from its surface planed

Its frigid eulogy, its grief of ice,—
Each awkward text, each weary dull device,
Dates, emblems, letters, all he did erase—
All save a lyre sculptured at the base—
Then glowing like the wisp that skips the moat,
A phantom epitaph the phantom wrote
In letters coldly luminous; it seemed
As if a glow-worm o'er the marble gleamed,
Creeping across it with his lantern green,
For each word vanished ere the next was seen:

"What is it in the garden of the Earth
If one bud wither, lovely though it be?
If one mind fails the promise of its birth,
What loss to man in man's Eternity?
This stone the type of cold rigidity,
This snow which noonday melts not, stands for one
Who deemed his mission was to feel and see;
For in him Nature's changing face was shown,
As seas and flowers change their aspect with the sun.

"Look down upon a plain of blooming flowers,
A forest, or the ocean, and behold
How these are grave or gay but as the hours
Which float above are clad in gray or gold—
Like these he changed, yet long ere he grew old
His heart became of one dull changeless hue;
The hedge 'twixt him and hopes, which childhood bold
A tussock deemed, a giant barrier grew—
Each year it seemed to gain in height and briers new.

"His was no sombre self-consoled despair
Which thinks the world as stupid as unkind,—

He deemed that he was wanting, and with care
He strove his nature's secret flaw to find;
He roamed o'er foreign lands and saw mankind
In many aspects, and with toil by night
He probed the thoughts of many a perished mind,—
By day he watched, all breathlessly, the fight
Which freedom ever makes against inhuman might.

"But as each hour adown time's chasm rolled,
Toil unrewarded wrought its vengeance dire—
His heart grew weary and his hand grew cold
In stirring the unfed, unwilling fire;
And as upon some lofty granite spire
The seeds, wind-wafted, lodging one by one,
With tiny thews which ages cannot tire
Hurl crumbling down each mighty sculptured stone,
So fell his noblest thoughts by petty cares o'ergrown.

"Oh, he was like a sprig of severed bay,
Whose functions perish ere its beauty cease,
Or like the smiles that o'er the features play
Of midnight sleepers, powerless to please,
And lost in darkness. 'Prived of rest and ease,
He could not frame his mind to sink, or soar—
His was obscurity without its peace;
For though life's winds his cloud-built empire tore,
Still phantom pageants swept his dazzled eyes before.

"Now all he was and all he strove to be,
All that he hoped that others might become,
Although recorded, none shall ever see—
Far better had he been forever dumb;
His hope of fame—"

       The spectre's hand was raised
More syllables to form, when sudden blazed
Athwart the ivy leaves' inwoven bar
The eternal radiance of a rising star—
Some thought of hope which lurked within the ray
Made the dim shadow's shadow fade away.
He faded fast, and left me standing there
Alone with Nature and relieved of care.
Thou silent witness that though crushed by ill
We are a part of something glorious still!
Sensation of expansion and expanse
Which lifts our thoughts above the fretful trance
Of our too subtle musings, the dull fear
That we but follow in the world's career,
The self-tormenting effort to be great,
How do these fade before thy tranquil state!
Oh, Nature, Nature, effortless and calm,
Thy beauty is the soul's eternal balm.

AUGUST.

I wandered through the chilly night,
  I heard the whip-poor-will,
The passing brant on high did chant,
  The frogs sang sharp and shrill;
And many a wild bird in his flight,
  With ghostly fall and swell,
To the far north, whence he came forth,
  Did hymn his wild farewell.

The Summer's cloak was faded,
  Her matron bloom was gone,
Her queenly pace had lost its grace,
  Her cheek was worn and wan;
But the moon as calmly waded
  The depths of the cloudless sky
As she did on the night when the queen was dight
  In the robes of majesty.

And I thought how the dews of even,
  As they gather on the brow,
May be made to gleam with the tingeless beam
  Of a light not born below—
How the glow from our inner heaven,
  With its sheen of deathless white,
May cast a ray on our senseless clay
  In the soul's eternal night.

TO THE DEAD IN THE SEA.

Mourn not, ye children of the sea, ye dead!
That no stone idly crumbles o'er your head—
The mounds that heave above your ashes are
As green as those o'er church-yard sepulchre,—
Yet who can mark their place? Is not each wave
An ever-green, far-rolling, restless grave?
Ye are not as the earth-bound dead, all still
And speechless; for I hear, with a wild thrill,
Your laughter mingle with the seethe and roar,
As fall the breakers on the midnight shore;
And as the foam gleams glistening through the night,
Your hands stretch out towards me ghastly white,
And clutching as to draw me to the sea—
What, would ye swell your vast fraternity?

TO THE WIND.

Eternal minstrel! who through every land
  Harpest wild melodies from door to door,
Thy lays 'neath palace eaves are not more grand
  Than in the smoky chimneys of the poor.

Saddest of harpers! of thy songs, can none
  Back to the lip a vanished smile recall?
No, there is not of all thy ditties one
  But wakes a sigh, or bids a tear to fall.
Thou singst of home to those that houseless rove,
  Past friends to those mankind despise and scorn,
Thy songs tell trembling age it once could love,
  And bid unwilling youth feel it shall mourn;

Thou singst of weed-grown graves with mossy stones
  Which we in life's rough race have left behind—
But thou dost not neglect them, and thy tones
  With kindred music wake the sleeping mind;

Thou singst of our own graves which thou shalt see,
  Of endless change which leaves thee still the same,
Of all we are not, and yet wished to be
  In brighter hours ere hearts and hopes grew tame.

Pilgrim impalpable! thy viewless feet
  Through ages still must roam from clime to clime,
But even thee at last a bourn shall greet—
  Thy head shall rest upon the tomb of Time.

AUTUMN LEAVES.

The leaves lie cold
On the cumbered mould,
Their corpses lie white all around,—
Uninterred where they fall,
Till their whiter pall
By Winter is spread on the ground;

But when March, with his cloud
And his voice so loud,
As he shouts in the leafless tree,
Shall lift with his hand
Their pall from the land,
The corpses shall vanished be.

A SONG OF YOUTH.

Middle-age, stand aside! on thy hopes there's a
  damper,
    There is cold in thy eye, there's a doubt in thy
      pace—
Stand aside from his path, lest the course thou
  shouldst hamper
    Of one who will die or succeed in the race.

He comes like the wind as it sweeps o'er the reeds
  Which cover the marshes so wide and so green;
He leans from his chariot and lashes his steeds,—
  Streaming backward his hair and his garments are
    seen.

There is heaven in his eye, there's a light on his brow,
  There's a curl on his lip, with the scorn of his pride.
As he cheers to his coursers his heart is aglow,
  And he sees not the being who clings to his side;

Fair, fair is her face as the pond lily's pure,
  As it floats o'er its grave in the depths of the
    stream—
Her glance is bewildered, half timid, half sure—
  She has fears for his danger and hopes for his
    scheme.

Swift as the dews of morning that fade in the loving
  light,
Swift as the words of warning we heard on a by-gone
  night,
    Swift as the spray
    That floats away
      Before him Fame doth fly—
    Her face is a vapor cold and gray,
      'Tis her back enchants his eye.

Let him on till he win her, and then he will find
She is dust on the billow and chaff on the wind—
Let him on till he win her, and then he will know
How vain the best efforts of mortals below.

Trembling Age, halt away with thy cane and thy
  crutch,
    There's a film on thy eye, on thy cheek sits decline—
Away! in his pathway a feather is much,
    And he needs all his strength, without hindrance
      of thine.

MORNING.

BEHOLD, the Morn, pale daughter of the Sun,
From her deep dream within the east awakes—
A ray to gild her lattice has begun,
A fitful breeze her cloudy curtain shakes.

A deep-blue veil enshrouds her face serene—
In vapory folds her tunic floats afar—
A mantle, too, she wears of lightest green—
Her rosy feet rest on the morning star.

Within her hand a crystal cup she holds,
From which she ever flings the tingeless dew,
Whose magic might each drooping bud unfolds,
Bathing the waking world in beauty new.

Her friends the flowers uplift their pearly heads,
And breathe a blessing as she passes by—
Their new-born breath upon the light wind treads,
And wreathing upward, melts into the sky.

The pale cold thoughts of wisdom, doubts of joy
Which doth not turn his burning eyes above,
Longing for endless fame, and glimpses coy
Of things for which in vain the mind hath strove,

These wait on her; and now to earth again
   She sends these forms which flit about her urn—
They knock a moment at the hearts of men,
   Then hasten upwards never to return.

The glowing stars, her flocks of golden fleece,
   She, their fair shepherdess, doth drive away
Westward across the far horizon's crease,
   And follows from our sight—But lo, 'tis day.

SONG.

THE moon with her viewless hands,
  Transparent, light and free,
    Was parting a place
    For her dreamy face
  To gaze on the troubled sea.

There were bells in wave-washed hands,
  Which tolled eternally;
    There was roar on roar,
    Far down the shore,
  And laughter out to sea.

There were four on the sands to-night,
  Two shadows and two forms—
    Behind and before
    Flew the froth on the shore,
  And foam on the land of storms.

Need shadows, or shapes more light?
  O which has the firmer home?
    Which stabler stuff,
    The moth-like fluff,
  Or the bird-like flying foam?

O heart-uniting kiss!
　O bosoms beating free!
　　O eyelids wet
　　With joy; and yet—
　The wild bells out to sea!

Through the languor of the kiss
　Which wrapped them tenderly,
　　Came the steady roar
　　Far down the shore,
　And the laughter out to sea!

THE SONG OF THE SHELL.

Down, down in the depths of the deep blue sea,
　Far from the home of the spray,
In the stillness of eternity
　For ages I dreamily lay.

And the pale sea-flowers that round me drank
　The light that crept through the brine,
Year after year arose and sank
　Seen by no eye but mine;

And the ships above through the depths profound
　Sent shadows with faces gray,
Who afraid of the dimness that threatened around
　Stole o'er us and crept away;

And far above us the fishes passed,
　Like shades when the sky is dim;
But we heard not the tramp of the waves as they
　　　massed,
　Nor the hurricane's battle-hymn.

The sunbeams swam down to us spent and pale
　Ere they reached our distant home;
But the moonbeams scorned our quiet vale,
　And slept on the eddying foam.

But the sibyl who dwells in the midst of the flood,
  The soul of the changing deep,
On her way through her realm before me stood,
  And roused me from my sleep;

And over my back she dimly traced,
  In a running and watery hand,
Strange letters in lines that each other effaced,
  Like the ripples that seek the sand.

"Ye are the leaves of the ocean," she said,
  "The sibylline leaves of the sea—
Go forth from the haunt of the graveless dead,
  Washed wide by the foam in its glee.

"And darkly forever recall to man
  With thoughts of your boundless home,
The gulfs on each side of his own slight span,
  The infinites past and to come."

She tore me away from my parent rock,
  But fast to this weed I clung—
Long was I tossed with many a shock,
  And here at last was flung.

SONNET TO THE HOURS.

YE motley throng that pass before mine eyes,
  Onward, still onward, unreturning crew,
  Of every size, of every shape and hue,—
Some smiling, and from lips like morning skies
Breathing the laughter soft of Paradise,—
  Some stalking by with faces dead and blue,
  While round our steps ye sprigs of cypress strew
In ghastly silence—why, alas, some prize
Do ye each, all, bear from us? Leaf by leaf
  Youth's stalwart tree ye take away, and blast
Hope's unripe fruit and Joy's half-garnered sheaf,
  Until so little there is left at last
To tempt you forth from out your secret home,
'Tis strange the last stern hour should ever come.

SAUL

A DRAMATIC POEM

PREFACE.

As the view taken by the author of the relations between Saul and his subjects is not, perhaps, the most common one, a word or two in explanation seems requisite.

It is plain, from the Bible account, that the priests were very unwilling to grant the people's clamorous demand for a king. It seems probable that in selecting Saul, a poor shepherd boy, they chose one whom they thought it would be easy to mould to their will. On finding himself firmly seated on the throne, however, far from being pliant and yielding, he showed an evident intention of substituting kingly for priestly rule. A struggle thereupon began, which ended only with Saul's life. Steadily the quarrel increased in violence and fury until it culminated in Saul's putting to death great numbers of the lower order of priests, together with witches, prophets, and the like, as being the mouthpieces and agents of the higher priesthood. The natural answer to this was a declaration that the kingdom had passed from Saul, and the secret anointing of another, in order to give a figure-head to the clerical party. Warned by their past experience, the priests chose in David a youth of a deeply religious mind, in whom afterwards all their hopes and wishes were fulfilled.

It is uncertain whether the Philistines were induced to make their invasion by direct solicitation, or merely by the unsettled state of the kingdom. In any case, the presence of David in the Philistine camp, and the fact that he would have taken part with them in the battle against Israel had it not been for the doubts of the Philistines on the score of his fidelity, show very clearly that the sympathies of the sacerdotal party were with the invader.

The scorn that Michal felt for David's religious superstition, and which burst forth in after-years, when he danced before the ark,* is no small confirmation of my idea that their education had been as different as possible. And David's ungenerous and weak reply, when he taunts Michal with her father's downfall and his own elevation in his stead, shows plainly that David felt it was to the very bigotry which his wife despised that he owed his crown.

My clue to the character of Phalti is found in II. Samuel, chap. iii. 16.

The story of the last days of Saul, as told in the Old Testament, has enabled me to practically preserve the unities without effort. I have taken the liberty of departing from the biblical text in so far only as to permit Saul's armor-bearer, in the last scene, to die before his master, and thus avoid a palpable anti-climax.

---

* II. Samuel, chap. vi. 14-22.

DRAMATIS PERSONÆ.

SAUL, King of Israel.

DAVID.

ABNER, Captain of the Host.

PHALTI, an officer.

JONATHAN,
ABINADAB, } Sons of Saul.
MELCHI-SHUA,

Ghost of Samuel.

MICHAL, Saul's daughter, who has been previously taken away from David, her first husband, by Saul, and given in marriage to Phalti.

The Witch of Endor.

Attendants, soldiers, etc.

The action of the drama is confined to Mount Gilboa and its immediate vicinity. Time, a single night and part of the following morning.

SAUL.

ACT 1.

SCENE I.

Nightfall.—A lonely spot just within the Hebrew outposts near Mount Gilboa.

Enter DAVID, disguised as one of SAUL'S soldiers.

DAVID.

'Tis strange that I, who had to pass the guards
And run all hazards, should be here the first.
What if my messenger mischanced! I fear
Lest ill hath come to Jonathan—for Saul
Hath long half doubted him—That cannot be,
Else were I taken—Hark!—It is a step—(*hides*).
I know that shadow—Jonathan! 'Tis I!

They embrace.

JONATHAN.

Thy message reached me but an hour ago,
And scarcely could I find a fit excuse
To quit the council. Anywhere but here
Thy sight were happiness, but thou must know
That to be taken here is certain death—
Why art thou come?

89

DAVID.

Thou knowest why I come.
Thou art my earliest and my dearest friend,
And shall I see thee sink beneath a doom
Which overhangs and topples o'er thy head,
And stretch no hand to pluck thee to my heart,
Where only there is safety? Jonathan,
Twice hast thou saved my life from him who long
Has been the scourge of Israel, and now
I fain would save thee from him, that alone
He may receive the merit of—

JONATHAN.

No more!
I know thy wrongs are great, but so has been
The provocation,—not at first from thee—
Thy heart was far from the intentions vile
To thee imputed—Yet thou hast become
By slow degrees, through priestly influence,
The head and hope of all our factious foes.
How much I loved thee let this be the proof,
That I still love thee; for to see thee here
In open arms against us doth abate
Much of that girlish tenderness which made
Our boyhood's love a proverb to our friends.

DAVID.

Come with me, Jonathan!

JONATHAN.

I'll never come!

DAVID.

There is no time for argument, and yet
I do so fear to fail that I must plead—
Oh hear me, Jonathan, thou art allied
With one who is the enemy of God—
Fight not against the Lord, but fly the accursed!
Doomed from the day when Agag was not slain
At God's command, but blasted since he slew,
At Nob, Ahimelech, the holy priest,
And eighty priests beside—thou knowest his sins,
His heart-beats number them—Then fly with me!
'Tis noble to desert from wickedness.

JONATHAN.

Had other lips dared thus to speak of Saul
They ne'er had spoken more.—I'd have thee know
That Saul, if he were now, instead of king,
But a plain goatherd, would be still by far
The greatest man in Israel—

DAVID, *interrupting him.*

Why, Ay,
The greatest—nay, for though thou just hast said
Thou lovest me no more, I would not wound—
The fate of all allied to thee is fixed,
But thine still quivers—pause while there is time,
Think ere too late—wilt thou not join us?

JONATHAN.

No.

DAVID.

Art thou then bound forever to this cause
Forecrushed of God?

JONATHAN.

For this most noble cause
I fight unto the death with all save thee.

DAVID.

And I with all save thee.—Adieu!

JONATHAN.

Adieu!

Exeunt severally.

SCENE II.

A house within the Hebrew lines.

SAUL (*solus*).

This restless hush, this lull before the storm,
Lies heavy on my spirit. 'Tis a time
Without a form, a very nondescript,
Too still for bustling self-forgetfulness,
Too close to tumult for the calm of thought.

My past seems unfamiliar—if I turn,
My Future is a name and nothing more.
The Future do we make our fixed abode,
While its uncertainties are scattered wide,
Accepting them as constant—but so soon
As they unite and crystallize, and form
A crisis near at hand, all things beyond
Are blotted from our sight by this great doubt—
We can but strive to cross it.

Enter ATTENDANT.

ATTENDANT.

Good my Lord,
The captain of the host awaits without.

SAUL.

Admit him.

Enter ABNER.

To ABNER.

For the color of thy news
I see at best 'tis neutral, from thy face,
So do not preface it.

ABNER.

I have no news
In need of preface. Watches have been set
Far out on all the roads. I hear the foe
Is moving, and we soon shall know his mind.

SAUL.

Hast thou been forth amongst the tents, to learn
The temper of the men?

ABNER.

Our tribe is staunch
Because it is our tribe—nay, all are firm,
They all will face the foe—But David is
Beloved in Israel.

SAUL.

Ay, there it is!
This pebble-throwing boy, this priestly tool,
This thing of songs, this curious piece of cloth
Whose warp is craft, whose woof is bigotry,
Has won the rabble's heart before that I
Could lift their minds above him. Even now
They will not judge him, though he is arrayed,
An open rebel, with our enemies,
And on the march to slay his brethren.

ABNER.

Nay,
I hear he is not trusted by the foe,—
It is not certain he will fight with them.

SAUL.

It is as certain full as that he is
The cup from which the priests would hope to drink
This people's blood—their liberty—for that
Is their souls' blood.

SAUL.

O Samuel!

Despite thine order, thou wert once my friend;
And now when all, all whom I then did trust
Have turned my foes, be thou, though in the tomb,
Again a friend—Oh, speak some word of cheer!
Give me thy counsel what 'twere best to do.
With lukewarm troops, and hourly thinning ranks,
I must oppose the great and eager host
Of the Philistines—I am in despair.
That black, arch rebel, Jesse's son, hath joined
The forces of the foe; and gives it out,
False villain that he is, that even by thee
He was anointed. I can find no help
In visions, or in dreams, or prophecies—
(Things which I once did scorn, but covet now)
Oh, speak to me! say, whither shall I turn?
What shall I grasp at?

SHADE OF SAMUEL.

Wherefore come to me,
Seeing the Lord has left thee? Jesse's son,
Whom thou despisest, is to-night the king,
And thou a king but in our chronicles.
Because thou wouldst not execute God's wrath
On Agag, king of Amalek, this doom
Has fallen on thee. Furthermore, the Lord
Will Israel with thee deliver up
(Slaughtering his people to make way with thee,)
Into the hands of the Philistine host.

Abner.

                    Our priests, my lord, are men
Of holy life—

Saul, *not heeding him*.

           It maddens me to think
That should I fail, I shall go down to time,
Since priests are our historians, as the foe
Of my own people whom I lived to save,
Tricked out, besides, by sacerdotal hate.
It will be told how often I did come
To sue forgiveness, shedding many tears,
With ashes on my head, upbraiding loud
My froward heart. Had I but been more swift
To catch and punish, letting none escape—
Had I forgotten always they were men,
In seeing they were priests, the tide had turned—
'Tis but a step 'twixt opposite beliefs!
But as it was, the few I left but gained
Strength from the slain, and skulked among the
    tribes,
The poison-mongering victims of their cause.

Abner.

I never was a friend to many rites—
I am a plain man—yet I would not dare
Thus to revile our priests; they are the link
Betwixt us and Jehovah.

SAUL.

It is time
You went to your own tent to take some rest—
We move at break of day—

Enter hurriedly a messenger.

MESSENGER.

My lord the King,
A body of the enemy is now
Moving towards the mountain, as it seems,
To occupy the heights.

SAUL.

It must not be.
The advantage of position is with us—
It shall not be! Abner, thou wilt draw out
A thousand chosen men for instant march—
Phalti shall lead them, and to save delay
I go to him, to give him my commands.

Exeunt.

SCENE III.

MICHAL's *apartment in the same.* MICHAL *is seated,*
PHALTI *reclining at her feet.*

PHALTI.

Michal, my own, my darling, my beloved,
Fain would I linger here, and by thy side

Forget that ever there was war on earth.
It is enough to watch those amorous hands,
Veined to the very finger-tips; and mark
Each easy, idle, half-voluptuous pose—
When one loves thus, 'tis almost death to go.

MICHAL.

Think that the cause you fight for is to you
Most holy, and that soon you may return
Loaded with honors, and enjoy them long.

PHALTI.

'Twere easier far to tear myself away
From passionate entreaties to remain—
To forcibly unwind thy close-locked arms,
And steel my lips to every clinging kiss,
Than to go thus in calm propriety,
With this cold, mother's blessing on my head.

MICHAL.

'Twould pain me much to think that I could stand
Betwixt you and your duty.

PHALTI.

                              There it sounds!
This self-same note forever in my ears!
Duty thou art thyself, personified—

Forever calm, obedient to my will,
Wanting in nothing—save in being part
Of my whole life, and heart, and inmost soul.

MICHAL.

Long have I striven to be all you wish.

PHALTI.

We feel no need to strive when once we love.
I hoped to slowly, surely win my way—
'Tis not so now—I see the distant goal
No nearer than at first—You love me not.

MICHAL.

Phalti, you do me wrong.

PHALTI.

            It may be so—
But still I do not see you deeply blush
When I come in, and pale when I depart.

MICHAL.

Push me no further—I cannot control
The mounting and descending of my blood.
To love you is my duty—

PHALTI.

What, again?
Accursed be the phrase, I almost said
Cursed be the lips that uttered it! And thou!
Dost thou suppose I deem thee so demure,
So cold, so calm, so breezeless? Nay, I know
Passion is there, too much, though not for me—
I know thy idle longings where they run.
And is it not enough that thou hast come
Straight from that renegade, that rebel—?

MICHAL.

Stop!
Trench not upon the past, or I may prove
That I can wake and speedily atone
For all my past docility—

PHALTI.

And I
Will prove my might, which fondness has concealed.

Enter SAUL.

SAUL.

Phalti, away! There is no time for words.
Go straight to Abner's tent; there thou wilt find
Men, guides, directions—Occupy and hold
The heights on Mount Gilboa.

PHALTI.

Yes, my Lord.

Exit, PHALTI.

SAUL.

Would more were like thee, Phalti! If I had
But a few score such soldiers, ere the moon
Can light yon mountain side my foes were dead,
All cut to pieces in a night surprise,
And that vile rebel—But I have them not—
And so, dear Michal, do I turn to thee,
Thee, a weak woman, yet my flesh and blood,—
And therefore in thee only shall I find
That sympathy with me and all my aims,
That reflex of my thoughts, which I must have.
Abner is but a soldier, and the rest
Are cowed by priestcraft into doubt and fear.
But I have formed thy mind, and I have forged
All thy soul's weapons for the war of life.—
Now, for I scorn concealment, when my fate,
Our fate, our cause stands in most desperate doubt,
The cause I've taught thee in our happy walks,
The cause I live for, I come home to thee—
Give me a hearty wish for my success,
And hurl a curse upon my enemies.

MICHAL.

You say most truly that you formed my mind,
I could not think against you if I would—
A handiwork must act within the laws

Of him who framed it. Need is none to ask
My mind's support, it is already yours.
Your cause is just, since surely it is right
To check the dark dominion of the priests—
And yet a cloud upon my spirit hangs,
I walk confused within a misty maze.
It seems to me there is some strange mistake,
That could you only meet with some of those
Who now oppose us, you would find them far
Less stubborn than you deem, that they would see
The splendor of your majesty and might,
And hasten to obey—Oh, think what joy
To be once more united all in love!

SAUL.

Your husband, it would seem, has little part
In these your dreams of happiness to come.
There is a ring of treason in your words.

MICHAL.

There is no treason to you in my heart.

SAUL.

Then prove it straight by calling ruin down,
Signal, complete destruction, upon all,
Without distinction, who oppose me now.

MICHAL.

May the Philistines suffer rout.

SAUL.

Well done!
I marvel at your warmth in my behalf!
What, as I entered, was the cause of strife
Betwixt you and your master, my beloved,
My well-tried Phalti?

MICHAL.

Ask my master that—
Lord Phalti best can tell on his return.
He was complaining, if my memory serves,
That I was far too meek and dutiful.

SAUL.

Lord Phalti! And you will not curse my foes!
Then naught remains for me but now to hurl
My curse on you; and tell you, since your heart
Is with that rebel, I will pluck it thence,
Though I uproot you with it, root and branch!

Exit SAUL.

ACT II.

SCENE I.

A moonlight balcony.

SAUL (*solus*).

Of all the shadows midnight and the moon
Upon me cast, none equals that within.
Would it were always night, a moonless night,
And I and all men isolated parts
Of universal shadow.—What are men?
Vain children plucking at the sleeve of Time,
Who stalks away unheeding. Once I deemed
The world was made for me to revel in.
Beauty was life's wide atmosphere, the breath
And essence of existence, ne'er to fail.
Joys poured so thick upon me, that my soul
Feared only lest, with all her granaries,
She could find room through life but for the tithe.
But soon I made a grand discovery—
That life was labor, and still happier so,
That happiness sprang only from renown,
And naught could satisfy, save leading men.
My sensual dream was fair, and if, indeed,
Its colors faded when too closely scanned,
It still gave pleasure; but ambition's dream
Was deadly, for within me lurked success.

Although those near in blood and far in heart
Tramped o'er the garden of my soul, it still,
By Obstinacy tended, bloomed the more.
But happiness before me flitted on;
For when the shepherd boy had won the throne,
Another vista opened out beyond,
And a new goal, though this time more defined.
I longed to turn my studies to account,
And make a nation of disjointed tribes;
To stifle superstition, and teach men
To be themselves the judges of their lives.
And still the more my thoughts grew absolute,
And abstract, and unpliable, the more
I deemed mankind were following close with me,
Till insurrection shook me by the arm,
And I awoke, and found myself alone.—
What is it to be in a wilderness?
Its thickly whirling leaves, or blowing sands
Speak with eternal voices—But to be
Alone in thought, to bear a gift to men,
And be waved off by every heart in turn,
Is desolation. To escape the frowns
Of those around me, I could wish my heart
Were leprous as their own. Wrapped in great
    thoughts,
From lack of sympathies, I shrank from men—
What agony to see them shrink from me!
Had I but loved the beings whom I saw!
Yet no one ever loved both man and men.
Then why not make my utter loneliness
But serve my greatness? It were nobler, sure,
To find in enmity the very oil
To make my zeal burn brighter than before—

A hundred times repeated, still the words
Sound cold and dead, and quickly float away,
Like echoes on the wind. Man cannot live,
Noble or vile, without the love of man.
All strive for it, and strive for that alone,
Beneath a thousand names and thousand masks.
A few of us, more daring than the rest,
Finding but little ready to our hand,
Pluck from the clouds the vapors of our choice,
And in far-flashing but uncertain tints
Trick out the wraith we call Posterity.
We clasp our misty doll, a moment glad—
But fading soon, it takes the ashen hue
Of all things else, and mingles with the air,
And leaves us staring stupidly around
For aught to clutch at, looking but in vain.

A sentinel passes, chanting slowly.

> The world's asleep—
>   Sleep on!
> My watch I keep
>   Alone.
> Toil, care, and crime
> Take breathing time—
>   Sleep on!

These varied phrases will not lift one flint
Of all the mountains pressing on my back,
So strong the sense of my identity,

From inward isolation, that it seems
That all the world must live or die with me.
E'en Time upon me lays his withered hand,
And moves but as I move, and holds me back—
Forever-more beside my hapless steps
Walk sorrow, mad confusion, and despair!

Sentinel repasses, singing.

Hearts o'er the world,
Care's sails are furled,
    Sleep on!
I vigil keep
That ye may sleep—
    Sleep on!

Leaves shuddering lisp
    On high,
Ghastly the wisp
    Hops by,—
Yet do not fear,
Sweet rest is here,
Vexed heart, thy troubles cease;
    Sorrows, away!
    Till break of day—
These be the signs of peace.

My mounted wishes I on foot pursue,
Their doubling tracks my guide across the waste;
But now their very traces disappear,
And I am doubting if they ever were
Aught but the hurrying squadrons of a dream.

A second sentinel passes, singing.

> The first watch wanes; the moon now dim,
>   Now bright, is sailing high—
> The first watch wanes, night's swallow grim
>   In the moonlight eddies by.

Is it so late? 'Tis time that they were here,
My messengers returning from their search—
A noble search! I hear their steps—Come forth!

(knocking heard within.)

Enter an attendant.

To attendant.

Well, have ye found the witch?

ATTENDANT.

                                     We have, my Lord.
A shepherd showed us where the sorceress,
Not far from Endor, dwells within a cave
High on the mountain; to the foot from here
Is scarce an hour's ride—Shall we then send
A squad to take her?

SAUL.

                                     No, I go myself.
I long have felt a wish, or rather whim,
From merest curiosity, to see
Some witch like this, of real force and fame,
In her own den, begirt with all her spells.—

Haste, bring the steeds. We must be back before
The dawn's first pale, sleep-smothered blush appear.

Exeunt attendants.

So wild a venture upon such a night,
The headlong gallop and the dizzy climb,
And all so close to the Philistine lines,
Will clear my brain and set my nerves at rest.

Exit.

SCENE II.

A mountain near Endor. Time, midnight. SAUL *and
two attendants mounting upward.*

SAUL.

The white and sheeted ghosts of the dead storms
Sweep by in majesty! and all around
The trees' dark branches seem to beckon me;
And near my path their rough and twisted roots,
Like coiled-up serpents, seem about to hiss;
And even the shadows, those most shapeless things,
Take living shapes about my fevered steps (*looking
    upward*).
Ye curling forms fantastical aloft,
Is it that hanging thus 'twixt earth and sky
I feel your influence, or are the sprites
Which now I seek, though unbelievingly,
Part of this stable world as well as I?

ATTENDANT, *coming up from below.*

My liege, we pray you hold! you climb so swift
That we, though straining, fall behind—we fear
To lose you in the darkness.

SAUL.

                          Ye are slow.
Yet will I pause upon this jutting crag
Whose edge invites me to its crumbling brink—
'Tis a most dizzy rock—beneath I see
The red and dotted camp-fires of our host,
Like fire-flies in the amorous month of June,
Flash as the breezes lift them.

ATTENDANT.

                          My good lord,
If it should please you, we will hasten on,
And strive to find the entrance to this cave.

SAUL, *not heeding him.*

A feather falling from such height 'twould seem
Might crush a tower to atoms. Far away,
Across the wide and lake-besprinkled plain,
The moonbeams kiss the waters into life
As radiant as their own. This glimpse beyond
The world that lives in contact with our steps,
This sudden outlook on a wider scene,
Blots out my narrow life of strife and pain;

Conspiracy and priestcraft, civil broil,
Shrink to their wraiths, and now become to me
But quaint, cold names of things of long ago.
My pristine purity, my early thoughts,
The passionate thoughts of heaven-gazing Youth,
Which soared aloft and left me in those days,
On reascending, lo! I find them here.
Why have I made them wait for me till now?
Let me believe reality is dead—
It seems so here—that I am once again
A boy upon Mount Ephraim, these pure beams,
These shadows, and this lofty solitude,
My childhood's playfellows—

ATTENDANT, *from above.*

                              My Lord the King,
I pray you hang not o'er yon treacherous cliff,
Lest it should crumble. We but now have found
The cavern you are seeking—please you, come.

SAUL.

Push on, I follow. Your unmeaning tongues,
Your thoughtless babble, checking this fair scene,
Are, for the moment, the deep voice of Fate.

                                        Exeunt.

SCENE III.

A cavern in the mountain, arranged as an abode.

The WITCH OF ENDOR (*sola*).

WITCH.

Weary and lone, weary and lone. Alas!
How many nights in perfect loneliness,
And utter desolation, have I sat
In this grim haunt which even the hunter shuns!
How often have I left my door of boughs
Half open, that the bats which dwell with me
Might come and go!—this is to be alone.
I, feeble, timid, and oppressed with years
Which I can scarcely reckon—I who need
The peaceful fireside, and the gentle hands
Of my descendants for my ministers,
Am driven hither by the fear of death,
To live a life far worse than death—What crime
Have I committed?—Is this criminal,
That at long intervals I have beheld
Shapes from the past and listened to the dead,
Becoming thus the mouth-piece of the tomb?
O Saul, O Saul, thou slayer of the priests
And scorner of the prophets, thou who hast
Destroyed my order, what wouldst thou perform?
Hopest thou to choke the accents of the grave?
The spirits speak not yet, but still I hear

Low whisperings, and I know thy hour is nigh—
Thy retribution comes—alas! alas!
Our nation's fortunes are with thine entwined.
Voices without, and sound of steps.
Oh God! they come to take me! Whither hide?
What, to be dragged forth like a badger? No!
Let them come on, I meet them here—Approach,
　　(*to those without*)
Whoe'er ye be, I wait within.
Enter, disguised, SAUL *and attendants.*

SAUL, *to his two attendants.*

　　　　　　　　Keep watch
And careful guard without 'gainst treachery.
They retire.
To the Witch.

Woman, whate'er thou art, thou sure must be
Or good, or ill, and this is, in itself,
No small distinction in this neutral world
Where few are either. I have heard thy fame,
And that to thee there is no past—I come
To exercise thy calling; and no time
Is mine to waste in prefaces—Call up,
From out eternity, the shape of him
Whom I shall name to thee. Nay, haste!

WITCH.

　　　　　　　　My Lord—
For though I know you not, your mien is high—
Come not to lay a snare for my old life,
It is not worth your pains. You know how Saul
Hath cut off all the wizards, and all those

Who dealt in witchcraft; therefore now depart,
Tempt me no farther, I would fain descend
Unsmeared with gore to my impatient grave.
'Tis now the only boon I ask of man.

SAUL.

It boots thee not to know who I may be—
But I possess great power with the king,
And now I swear that by the Lord of Hosts,
The God of Israel, no harm shall come
To thee for aught thou doest—haste, proceed!

WITCH.

Whom shall I call, my Lord?

SAUL.

                    Call Samuel.

WITCH.

Mighty prophet, from thy deep,
Dreamless, everlasting sleep,—
Even from nothingness awake,
And thy perished form retake.
Let such thoughts as need but soul
Join to make thy phantom whole—
Let my will transfused through thee
Gift thee with identity.
By the Covenant, and by
Its mighty ark of victory,
By the name which Hebrews prize,
Wake, dread spirit, wake, arise!

                              A pause.

SAUL.

Woman, thy earnestness might shake the doubt
Of weaker minds—What, hast thou seen a shape?

WITCH, *not hearing him.*

Dim forms are rising, even as when the wind,
That vaccillating sculptor, shapes the clouds,
Each form, half moulded, he in turn destroys
To rear the following—here are figures wild,
In gestures threatening, and in aspect fierce,
Yet most indefinite.

SAUL.

What see'st thou now?
Speak quickly, for my heart is in my throat.

WITCH.

'Tis changed, 'tis changed! an old man cometh up
Wrapped in a mantle, full of majesty—
The phantom mutters—Nay—O thou art Saul!
Oh, spare my life!

Shade of SAMUEL *appears.*

SAUL.

Peace, woman, thou art safe.
Grim shade of one in life most grim and stern,
But doubly ghastly now, I charge thee speak!

SHADE OF SAMUEL.

Why hast thou broke my trance, and called me back
To memory and pain?

SAUL.

O Samuel!
Despite thine order, thou wert once my friend;
And now when all, all whom I then did trust
Have turned my foes, be thou, though in the tomb,
Again a friend—Oh, speak some word of cheer!
Give me thy counsel what 'twere best to do.
With lukewarm troops, and hourly thinning ranks,
I must oppose the great and eager host
Of the Philistines—I am in despair.
That black, arch rebel, Jesse's son, hath joined
The forces of the foe; and gives it out,
False villain that he is, that even by thee
He was anointed. I can find no help
In visions, or in dreams, or prophecies—
(Things which I once did scorn, but covet now)
Oh, speak to me! say, whither shall I turn?
What shall I grasp at?

SHADE OF SAMUEL.

Wherefore come to me,
Seeing the Lord has left thee? Jesse's son,
Whom thou despisest, is to-night the king,
And thou a king but in our chronicles.
Because thou wouldst not execute God's wrath
On Agag, king of Amalek, this doom
Has fallen on thee. Furthermore, the Lord
Will Israel with thee deliver up
(Slaughtering his people to make way with thee,)
Into the hands of the Philistine host.

Thy joys and hopes, thy beauty and thy strength,
Thy friendships, and thy pleasures, and thy peace,
Thy better moments, and thy happier thoughts
Are in the past, and thou upon its verge.
To-morrow shalt thou be what I am now—
A terror unto all things, save thyself—
A concrete part of that great abstract, Death—
That one great mote which turns man's sight to
      tears,—
That dread negation, and that dull mistake.
Farewell! we part, I to my sullen sleep,
Thou to thy shuddering passage to the tomb.

As SAUL *falls fainting to the earth the scene*
    closes.

ACT III.

SCENE I.

MICHAL's *apartment.*

MICHAL (*sola*).

'Tis past the midnight hour, and yet methinks
I ne'er shall sleep again.—Their bitter taunts
At last have roused my soul, and fevered thoughts
In answer to their challenge come in crowds.
Phalti and Saul, if that ye had been wise,
Ye had not asked for more than I can give;
Or asking it, and seeing me in doubt,
Striving to live, yet longing but to die,
Ye had not sought to force the gates of love
By wearisome upbraidings or abuse.
A woman rarely wishes to be loved—
Misers at once and prodigals they are:
All love they fain would hold within themselves,
To squander all where least there is a chance
Of just return. And thus it is with me.
Had Phalti's been a less uxorious love,
Less constant and, I shame to own, less pure—
Perchance—But no, it might not, could not be!
I could not still be living, and forget
That beauty and that strength which taught me
        love—

Taught me to languish, and to die of joy,
My pulse to flutter, and my breath to fail—
Taught me to cease from thinking and to live!
O life all sense, all passion, and all soul,
O life of mad excitement full of rest,
'Twere better far to die than longer live
Without thee! Peace, wild heart, be still!
Think how that life was sapping to the mind,
Think—think of aught to help allegiance back!
Father, my duty surely is to thee,
What should I be, deprived of thy support?
Thou gavest me life, and hast endowed my mind,
And yet, since thou art father to my woe,
Perchance I owe thee naught—I cannot tell.
My conscience says that I should strive to feel
The worth of Phalti's love, that I should lean,
As once I leant, upon my father's arm—
And yet this is the most that I can do:
In sullen silence to tramp on alone;
Now turning back and gazing wistfully,
Now staggering on, instinctive, at the call
Of one or both; with mind and senses chilled,
With wavering heart, not fixed in either faith—

A breathing type of human misery.
Oh, it would help me in my bitter woe,
To know a day was coming, though so far
It should but seem a rear-ward speck of dust
Of the long caravan which ages lead
Across this desert world—a time when love
Might walk the earth, unchained and unreproached,
When woman's person might but follow free
Where'er her heart was guiding—Ah, I fear

This wingless, footless hour will come to us
No sooner than when Truth fantastical
Has grown a substance,—Sorrow a dim shade,—
Vain-longing ceased to be sustaining food,—
Death grown a harlequin, and Time a sloth.

Enter female attendant.

ATTENDANT.

My lady, have you heard the dreadful news?

MICHAL.

No, speak, what news?

ATTENDANT.

Perchance it is not true.

MICHAL.

I charge thee, by the Eternal, speak!

ATTENDANT.

Indeed,
It may not all be true—Pray do not look
So deadly pale—

MICHAL.

Speak now! unless—unless
You wish to see me die—

ATTENDANT.

Oh, hear it then!
They say there has been fighting near the heights,
And that he has been taken, if not slain.

MICHAL.

He, who?

ATTENDANT.

Lord Phalti, who else could I mean?

MICHAL.

Why keep me in such mad suspense and dread?
For I had thought—I mean I cannot tell—
I am bewildered—tell me all again.

ATTENDANT.

There's nothing more to tell.

MICHAL.

Did you not say
Lord Phalti had been slain?

ATTENDANT.

Taken, or slain.

MICHAL.

Tell me more facts—Did other leaders fall—
Leaders of our, or of the other side?

ATTENDANT.

None that I know of, lady—None, I think.

MICHAL.

I am bewildered—Leave me all alone—
Yet stay within my call.

ATTENDANT, *aside.*

              This heavy blow
Has stunned her and benumbed her senses quite.
                    Exit attendant.

MICHAL.

Freedom is freedom still, though bathed in blood!
This moment, out of all Eternity,
Is mine! The Past has risen from the grave!
I hear *his* voice—What answer shall I make?
Yes—No—yes—no—I must not, it is wrong—
Wrong! It is treason! Give me time to think.
Away with thought! Thought has but wrecked my
    soul.
Unsought the plan springs up before my mind.
Is it inspired, or is it but a black
And foul temptation? She will think I go,
Half crazed by grief, and led by wifely love,
To search for Phalti—When once past the lines!
Help, I am dizzy, help!
            The attendant enters and offers aid.
Commanding herself.
                  'Tis almost past,—
It was a moment's faintness, that is all.

Go to the sentry whom I lately saw
Pacing beneath my window—Give him now
All thou canst carry—offer him besides—
Worlds, should he ask them! Stick at nothing, so
He will consent to help us through the lines.

ATTENDANT.

Think of the peril, think how vain the search,
If my Lord Phalti has been taken—

MICHAL.

                      Go!
But one word more, one breath may cost thee—Go!
                          Exit attendant.
Oh, father, grieve not, think me not unkind,
Thou never wert so dear to me as now.
I go to draw thee to the one I love,
And him to thee; or failing that, to strive
To mitigate your violence.—And now (*goes to a
      burnished mirror*)
I leave thee, father, this poor lock of hair,
As a remembrance, till we meet again;
To show thee I depart in perfect love,
And in the hope—What madness!—Even now
I feel his eye consume me—'Tis in vain! (*sinks into a
      seat.*)
                        Attendant re-enters.

ATTENDANT.

The sentinel consents to let us pass.

MICHAL, *starting up.*

And help us?

ATTENDANT.

Yes.

MICHAL.

Pass on before, I come.
Exit attendant.

I cannot go—I cannot stay—and yet—
To feel his breath once more upon my cheek,
To pant upon his bosom—and then die!
O David, master, husband, I am thine!

Exit.

SCENE II.

*A desolate moonlit pass. A pale streak visible in the
east. Enter* MICHAL *wearily. Throws herself down
at the foot of a rock.*

MICHAL.

I can no more, and yet I still must on.
It all seemed plain and easy at the start;
When with unwearied limbs and soul unlost
I left my sheltering room, no longer mine.
I was, by some impossibility,
To be a link of love 'twixt two opposed
And mighty beings, both of whom I love.

I strove to be the bridge between two high
And frowning crags—I hurled myself across,
And have but fallen into the abyss
Which yawns between, that gulf, black, bottomless,
Through which I still am falling. What are limbs
Aching and bruised, and flint-chopped, bleeding feet,
And fevered head, beside the tired soul—
The dizzy, lost and homeless soul? Alas!
My freedom is but liberty to die;
For how can I before the man I love
Appear a foot-sore, draggled suppliant,
A wandering outcast, and a traitor, too?
I who was—Oh, it cannot be! and soiled,
Soiled in his eyes since those delicious days
When I was his, all his—Down, down, vile self,
Thou cold slug that dost sting the tree of life
Till it puts forth deformities. To doubt
The being I adore is base—I go (*rising*)
To seek him, trusting only to his love,
E'en though I should fall dead before his tent
Of weariness and shame—

Enter PHALTI, *wounded.*

Who's there? Ah!

She falls with a shriek to the earth.

PHALTI.

                              See,
'Tis only I—No foe is near—'Tis I,
Phalti, thy husband—Wake, belovèd, wake!

MICHAL.

It is some hideous dream—Oh pardon! Oh,
Let us part quickly ne'er to meet again—
But not in wrath—though I have done thee wrong,
Much have I suffered.

PHALTI.

                    Thy poor mind is dazed
By the mad fever of fatigue. Forgive!
'Tis easy to forgive one loved before
For this, that she has nobly fronted death,
And suffered hardship, just to search for me,
Who am not worthy to be found alive.
But if I live 'tis from necessity:
When all was lost I thought by my own hand
To die; but in a moment more I flung
My sword over the precipice, and shame
Kindled my cheek to think that I had planned
To make my death my screen, and slink away
From my plain duty to the King. In war
Misfortune is a crime. Saul did not say,
"Take thou the heights if those with thee prove true,
And bravely do thy bidding," but he said,
"Phalti, go thou and occupy the heights,
And hold them." I have failed—And now I go
To pay with my poor life this failure. Come!
My hours are numbered; and when I am gone
('Tis hard to say), perchance thy lot will be
Brighter and happier—Darling, come away.
Rest dost thou need, and I will lead thee straight
To thy fond father's arms—

MICHAL.

                         Not there! Not there!
Oh let me go, I say! Or kill me now!
Thou goest to death—and what is death beside
The thought of standing 'neath my father's eye?
To have him call me traitor, whom I love,
And tear my passion from my breast with scorn,
And trample it all bleeding under foot—
My love is thine, and I will worship thee
With heart and soul and sense and every nerve,
If thou wilt only let me go!

PHALTI.

                             This night
Has shattered thy poor nerves and turned thy brain.
Rest only can restore and calm thy mind;
Even against thy will thou must with me—
Come, dearest, come, I bear thee hence to peace.
          Exit, bearing with him the half struggling,
            half fainting MICHAL.

SCENE III.

MICHAL's *apartment.*

SAUL, *at the open window.*

The misty grays and violets of the dawn,
Last lingering remnants of the quiet night,
Are dying one by one, and in the east

The blood-red hue of this combative day
Comes flashing up and staining all the world.
The saddest is to think an hour hence
I shall enjoy the carnage, and be made
To undergo the influence I hate,
And imitate the stupid violence
Of the vile cause I combat. Fade away,
Fade sober tints, pure colors of the soul,
My clear, my mind-appealing cause must bear
The brutal arbitration of the sword.
First of the suns, if prophecy be true,
That shall behold my world a blank to me,
Thy rising which should bring me solemn thoughts,
Speaks only of the march, and nothing more.—
Strife never seemed so hateful as to-day,
Nor wrath so senseless; and yet here it was
I parted from my child with bitter words,
Unjust to her, the only one I love.
Michal, come forth! I know I did thee wrong,
I have but little to forgive, and thou
Hast more than I would own to—Hasten, child,—
Nay, do not sulk, indeed there is not time.
Thou hast been sharer in my inmost thoughts,
And now that we must part, and part, perchance—
Come, bid me speed—

An attendant enters.

ATTENDANT.

What would my Lord the King?

SAUL.

Thou must have heard—I would the princess—Go!

ATTENDANT.

The princess is not here—that is—I mean—
The captain of the host is here, my Lord.

SAUL.

What means this stuttering bewildered fool?

Enter ABNER.

Abner, where is my daughter?

ABNER.

She is fled.

Shall we pursue?

SAUL.

Ay, take her, if you will.
Set all the camp to grinding of their swords—
There's time enough, they need not quit their lines—
Tell them to sharpen to a wire-edge,
'Twill soonest reach the bone. Before thy tent
Bid Melchi-shua and Abinadab
And all the captains meet me, to receive
My final orders ere we storm the heights.

Exeunt.

SCENE IV.

The camp.

SAUL, ABNER, ABINADAB, MELCHI-SHUA, JONATHAN
(apart), *and captains.*

SAUL.

Captains, I have no flowers of speech for you,
No exhortations, no haranguing words
Of general meaning. All of you I know,
And love and trust you all. To-day we fight
For freedom; since this black Philistine host
Comes at the call of a vile faction, who
Would barter national liberty for power,
And fix a cursed oligarchy here,
A secret, dark and mystic tyranny;
Trampling to death that natural government,
That secular, free, open, mutual rule
Which ye yourselves have chosen.—Scale the heights!
Take quick advantage of each bush and twig—
Creep, shield your bodies with each jutting stone;
And when with care and toil ye gain the top,
Cut not your enemies, but pierce them through,
Exposing not your persons. And be sure
Where'er the stream of blood shall thickest rise,
Fantastically curling up on high,
There in the midst, like lightning in a cloud,
Shall ye behold the flashings of my blade.

And now farewell! Ye know your posts—Advance!
Abner, go with them—Soon we meet with joy,
Or meet no more.

ALL, *drawing their swords.*

Farewell!
Exeunt, except ABINADAB, MELCHI-SHUA, *and*
JONATHAN.

SAUL, *to* ABINADAB *and* MELCHI-SHUA.

Come here, my sons.
Ye two and Abner I can wholly trust;
But many of the captains are not sure,
And should the day go heavily with us,
Close in upon the wings, and swiftly lead
Your little remnants up to join with mine,
That we may make one push for victory,
Or perish side by side.

ABINADAB.

Yes, father.

SAUL.

Go!

Exeunt ABINADAB *and* MELCHI-SHUA.

To JONATHAN.

Some whom I most have trusted, Jonathan,
Have proved unworthy; should the converse hold,
Thou, whom I oft have doubted, now shouldst be
Our chief support.

JONATHAN, *advancing*.

      Try me, my Lord.

SAUL.

                But if,
In thick of fight, the man I would not name
Who has been made the nucleus of this storm,
Should meet thee, wilt thou kill or capture him?

JONATHAN.

The man you mean is not now with the foe.

SAUL.

Where heard you that? You know too much—
    Depart!
Keep near Abinadab throughout the fray,
And do your duty.

JONATHAN.

      You shall see, my Lord.

                     Exit.

SAUL.

She cannot hope for mercy, if brought back—
Could she not wait till I was in my grave!
And Phalti, too! but he at least is dead,
And she will not be taken while alive.
'Tis much to know I ne'er shall see them more.

     Enter MICHAL, *supported by* PHALTI

Phantoms, away! Accursed shadows, flee!
One have I wronged, yet both have me betrayed!
I dread ye not—Begone!

MICHAL, *feebly*.

                              Alas! my Lord,
We are not phantoms yet—Oh would we were!

SAUL.

I scarce can tell, ye look so worn and wan,
So inorganic, effortless and strange,
Ye seem but forms of human agony.
Things which a falling dew-drop might engulf,
Or gossamer might strangle, or the breeze
Dissolve, diffuse, and mingle with the air.
Curses I had for one of you, and death
Perchance for both, yet who can curse or kill
A lifeless shade which pain doth animate?
Speak, if ye may.

PHALTI.

                              My master, I am come
To offer up my life, of little worth,
Save as a pledge of my fidelity,
Now forfeit through my failure.

SAUL.

                              Get thee gone!
Thou hast destroyed our cause, and ruined me,—
Thy sight is hateful,—yet I do not know
Of one just reason for thy death—Begone!

Phalti.

Scarce need I recommend to your kind care
My wife, your daughter, whom I lately found
Searching for me within the pass—

Saul, *interrupting him.*

Why, ay,
She searched for thee, and hoped to find thee dead,
And, dead or no, to slake and satiate
Her frantic passion for thy foe—At last
Thou goest forth, uncertain, dizzy, blind,
Drunk with thy sorrow.

Turning to Michal.

But where goest thou?
There is no place in Heaven or Earth for thee.
Help, some one help! She falls! Michal, my child!
Michal, my darling—Ah! 'tis but a swoon—
I thought her dead.—Thou hast the self-same look
Thou hadst that day in childhood when I found
Thee sleeping softly by the rivulet,
Thy tiny hand still grasping tiny shells,
And thy hair crowned with weeds—No more I see
The passionate kisses of my enemy
Upon thy altered lips. If thought there be
After this life—within the land of shades,
Purged of thy passion, be thou unto me
Companion of Eternity! Farewell! (*a distant trum-
pet sounds.*)

As Saul *rises from his knees and moves away,
the scene closes.*

SCENE V.

Mount Gilboa.

Sounds of battle and pursuit. Enter SAUL *and his armor-bearer, both mortally wounded.*

ARMOR-BEARER.

Here may we pause. Behind these rocks we stand
Out of the current of the flying—

SAUL.

                                        Ay!

Out of the current of the world we stand—
Time hath passed by us, leaving me to creep
As best I may, into my bloody grave.

ARMOR-BEARER.

There is no hope for any of us now.

SAUL.

My sons are dead—all three—Abinadab
Died fighting desperately when all his wing
Were broken, mixed and flying; after him
Fell Melchi-shua, noble in despair;
And Jonathan, whom I did half suspect,
Died best of all in that last furious charge
Which almost saved our fortunes.—

ARMOR-BEARER.

        Hark! I hear
The sound of horses' hoofs.

SAUL.

        It is the foe
Close on the heels of those who passed just now—
I would not die by these Philistine dogs—
Take thou this sword and hold it steadily—
Nay, hold it true—for I have had enough
Of suffering already.

ARMOR-BEARER.

       My good Lord,
I am bewildered—There, will this then do?
      Holds the sword feebly.

SAUL.

What, trembling so?

ARMOR-BEARER.

      I cannot help it—no,
      Lets fall the sword.
I cannot do this deed—I do not know
Whether it be because thou wert the King—

SAUL.

I *was?* nay, thou art right, I was the King.

ARMOR-BEARER.

It may be these deep wounds—for I am faint—
I cannot see thee, Saul, this dizziness—
      Faints and dies.

SAUL.

Now I am left to finish it alone.
Mere pain were nothing—But to kill the world
Of thoughts within, collected through long years,
Result of toil, of pleasure, and of pain—
A world so multitudinous that I
Think only of the havoc I must make!

Pauses.

Why should I writhe thus—am I not alone?
The sounds of the pursuit have swept afar,
And left me like a stranded broken shell,—
It is so silent and so peaceful here
The time seems altered, and the work quite done,
And Saul and all his miseries a tale
Heard long ago in childish years, as told
In dreamy accents o'er a hearth of coals,
Whose shapes fantastic acted out the play—
My mind is wandering, yet I cannot now
Command it back to face reality.
The myriad tribes and peoples of the earth, *(deliri-
ously)*
A writhing mass of passions, efforts, wills,
With only love of self distinct and clear,
That cause of all their good and all their woe,
Calm, passionless, removed, I see them now,
As the much-pondering, absent-minded moon
Looks down upon the nations of the clouds.

Sounds of the Philistines close at hand.
The bitterness is back again! Away!

Falls upon his sword.
My thoughts disband, for they are homeless now.

Dies.

THE LAST CRUSADE

A SATIRE

" The patron of true Holinesse
Foule Errour doth defeate."

NEW YORK—1873

CANTO FIRST.

IF, reader, like to me, you've lost a leg,
And since thro' life stumped sadly on a peg,
I know before the limb was amputated,
For hours in an office damp you waited,
Nor would the severed member's acquisition
Alone suffice the greedy quack physician.
All must be paid for in this age of ours—
Kind looks, soft words, sweet music, and bright
     flowers.
'Tis a fast age! Swift Progress hurrying on,
Has distanced Art, and Nature far outrun.
Fair Nature's face in sylvan solitudes
I've sought to read, and there, "where none intrudes,"
Tried to refresh my worn and weary soul
By contemplation of the mighty whole.
But when I wander by the lonely strand,
And watch the breaking billows sift the sand,
A bobbing buoy dancing 'midst the spray,
From lofty musings turns my mind away,
And tells me that in Blank Street, number nine
I'll find an undertaker quite divine.
Or, if inclined to rove by woodland rills—
I'm told a novel remedy for chills.
In those deep shades, where nymphs with satyrs
     twined
Their graceful dances, while the murmuring wind
Made cadence for their lightly falling feet,
Far other sights and sounds the senses meet.

Now advertisements bend the groaning trees,
And sign-boards creak with every passing breeze;
Each fruitful bough its magic nostrum bears,
On every stone a hieroglyph appears.
Where rustic shepherds purest pipings played
On oaten reeds, till their wild warblings made
The air all melody, the factory's whistle
Now shakes the very down from off the thistle:
I've given up seeking Pan thro' copse and thicket,
And pay five dollars for my opera-ticket.

Not long ago, Vice was a monster hideous,
But now she's grown a maiden most insidious;
Then all might pelt, and all might freely rail,
And Pope e'en tied a kettle to her tail;
But now a fair, so blushing, shy, and tender,
We hire scores of writers to defend her,
Who call her Virtue—truth, she's so demure,
One scarce can tell the vicious from the pure.
Indeed, one hardly dare abuse her, fearing
To wound the gentle wicked within hearing;
Perhaps, too, diving down a little deeper,
The reason men thus sacred strive to keep her,
That no rough stave her tender ribs may batter
She's crept too near our homes, we dread the clatter.
Thus, when young Harry his new apron tears,
Grave pater whips the child and loudly swears;
But should his daughter cut some sorry caper,
For him and his she soon becomes a vapor—
A shade, a blank—her name is never mentioned,
Tho' she live near, oft seen, and even pensioned.
Indeed, distinctions are become so nice
'Twixt comely virtue and 'twixt ugly vice,

'Twixt unbelievers dire, believers true,
That I am quite bewildered—are not you?
Sad heretics are gathered in a fold
To hear the gospel—should the converse hold,
Believers will be scattered far and wide.
But I, unskilled in argument, have tried
To lead my camel-Pegasus o'er sands
Perchance not trod by all our Bedouin bands,
By thoughts of naught but paltry booty led.
Wrapping my Muse's mantle round my head,
And humble in my posture, I have made
Some refuge from the parched simoom of trade.

Their caps in air see Unitarians toss,
Yet cower within the shadow of the cross,
Like warlike sheep that o'er the meadows stray—
Aggressive, seeking for some joust or fray;
But if a helpless puppy cross the mead,
Baa, stamp their silly feet, and then stampede.
Too vain to fight 'neath Christians' banners tattered,
And don their plumeless helms and corselets battered;
Too timid to enlist where thoughts arrayed,
Meet dogmas hand to hand and blade to blade
Like true camp-followers hanging in the rear—
Base, ragged scullions, swift to shout and cheer;
Afraid to fight, the scum of either side,
Ever prepared to flee, they skulking hide.

See Trinity's tall champion mount the pulpit,
And toss his arms, and shout as if a bull-pit,
Not church, surrounded him, and he would fain
Excite the bull, or haply stun his brain;
But when the inspiration has run low,

And turbid rhetoric no more will flow,
Looking to see where so much noise began,
We find a vain and rather fat young man.
So streams high swollen by late heavy rains,
With muddy waves o'erflow the adjacent plains,
But soon return to obscure and hidden nooks,
And end at last in naught but babbling brooks.
Slippers and silver rings his flock bestows—
The rings he well might wear within his nose;
One foot at least a slipper bright had known,
If all might melted be and poured in one.

Poets we have—a single poem? no—
For as *one* swallow makes not summer, so
A *thousand* janglers make not poetry,
Tho' all thrive well, and some may chance to see
A fifth edition, having learned that *whining*
Will serve their turn, and rhyme full well with
  dining.
If I were good at similes, I'd make
A long one now, and liken to a lake
Our literature—a vast, dull, waveless sea,
Whose very ripples wander wearily;
And which, tho' tideless, slowly ebbs away,
Still sinking thro' its ooze—an inch a day.
Here view the native fisher-poets, sailing
All lazily from bank to bank, and baling
Their crazy skiffs, still floundering on, and fishing
With tangled lines and nerveless arms, all wishing
To catch naught but the speckled populace,
That roves in monstrous shoals from place to place.
And, strange to say, these fishes ne'er grow wary,
Nor need the fishermen their bait to vary.

Each fish, like Peter's haddock, bears a penny
Within its mouth—the poet throws, and when he
Has brought one up, he holds the wriggler fast,
Extracts the piece, then makes another cast.

You cry, "I grant that poetry is waning;
But mourn her not, and cease this harsh complaining,
Great Science, now." . . . Can Science' light on high
Atone the loss of Art and Poetry?
Tell me, thou mariner! when the wild wave
Sweeps o'er thy vessel, and no hope may save—
Slow sinking, dost thou turn thy imploring gaze
On the cold moon, still struggling thro' the haze?

I hate all those that fain would desecrate
High poetry, and all that dare to rate
It 'mongst the arts, and say 'tis skill in words.
Will bunched-up feathers, then, make voiceful birds?
And does no throbbing heart, no bounding sprite
Inspire the lark by day, the owl by night?
And has, then, Poetry no breathing soul—
No rush, no flush, no flood beyond control?
Will care and study passioned thought inspire?
Thy tongs may stir, but will they light the fire?
I loathe, detest, despise these mean detractors—
Let them leave poesy and turn contractors.
Men not of genius but of talent talk so,
Because their aims their little means will balk so.
For me, I write with heart as well as hand,
Tho' they that feel not fail to understand;
And if I follow tears with merriment,
Or merriment with tears, I ne'er repent
My vanished mirth, nor mock my tears—I write

The only world that meets our mortal sight.
'Twere tedious, too, to laugh for years together,
And even sneers would turn the lip to leather.
Sit for long months beside your dead friend's grave,
And as they pass, with tears the new grass lave;
And when you have been mourning all this while,
He'll come up an anemone—and smile.

I am as one of many waves that lash
The sterile strand of Time; which, tho' they dash
In fragments, break not silently; the ear
Can ne'er forget of him that once shall hear
These boisterous voices of Eternity—
The waves still roll, still break, yet are the sea!
And tho' I be but a faint ripple, yet,
Ere the next wave o'ersweeps it, I would fret
My little wavering ridge upon the shore,
And murmur on, though drowned amidst the roar!

Here, reader, pause: and if you can, oh! calm a
Little your haste, for I a panorama
Would here display, without much true connection
An author's portrait gracing every section.

In Mediocrity's vast mausoleum
(Ye pilgrims of the great bathos go see 'em),
Two monumental slabs may be discovered
Half buried, and with dust and cobwebs covered.
These tombs in naught but their inscriptions vary;
The one bears "Phillips," and the other "Cary";
And touching them, deep in the humblest grotto,
Appears a third, bearing this curious motto—

Fame's Vaunted Laurel's naught but Prickly
     Holly;
And underneath is written, Little Olly.
The public here interred him—let him rest.
By ill-digested *breakfasts* he's oppressed
No more; his useless toils have ceased for ever:
Now hear how fate his thread of life did sever.

Parnassus rose before me, his dark brow
Clear cut against the evening sky; a glow
From the far sunset hallows round his head—
A tribute from the dying to the dead.
The sun's red disk is set, yet all is light,
Save in the mountain's shadow. But a sight
Unnerves, confuses, almost strikes me mute.
Behold! look! see! far down there at the foot,
A druggist's shop! where streams of light shine thro'
Vast colored bottles; but its sign-board new,
To read aloud my tongue almost refuses—
"O. W. H., Physician to the Muses."
But who is he that down the mountain side
Comes slowly, with a trembling step? while pride,
A god-like pride, upon his wasted face
Contends with fell disease. But look! his pace
At sight of me he strives to mend; I'll go
And ask him of this sign—perchance he'll know.
"Hail! noble sir; for haply you can tell,
What means yon hateful placard in the dell?"
"Stranger, my name's Apollo—nay, arise,
None this thin face and form could recognize;
I've been so swilled and drenched — nay, drowned
     with physic.
I really fear I'm falling in a phthisic.

The Muses, too, have suffered from yon fellow;
Poor things! they're sadly changed, all wan and yel-
    low.
If they're the least bit lively, or splenetic,
This quack prescribes a versified emetic;
And should imagination's flush o'erglow 'em,
They quick receive a mild cathartic poem.
A cold infusion of nonsense the chief part,
However, of his practice is; the heart
Is paralyzed; but look! on his own sill
The villain stands; a single shaft would kill
The wretch; I'd shoot him even now,
If some kind friend would only string this bow,
For I'm too weak—pray, sir, will you not try?"
I took the bow, and, straining mortally,
Till I could hear my muscles fairly crack,
The weapon partly strung, and gave it back.
And now the god receives the half-strung bow,
Draws a deep breath, and with a motion slow
Fits the bright arrow; while his careful eye
Computes the distance which the shaft must fly
To reach the doctor where he grinning stands,
Lolling the tongue, and pointing with his hands.
One quick, convulsive effort, to the head
Draws the long reed—twang—see! the shaft is sped;
E'en now it pierces *Olly's* massy skull;
He staggers, reels, and falling with a dull,
Strange sound, he supine rolls upon the earth,
And floods of frothy poems vomits forth;
While inky streamlets spreading o'er the sward,
And gathering volume, in Cephissus poured
So fast his waters gained upon the ground,
I fled in haste, to escape from being drowned.

Next view Columbia's poet pioneer—
If lines make poets, boots a mountaineer;
Speaking bad grammar, too, as if he sought
To show how poor the rhymes of men untaught,
And warn his brother woodsmen, lest that they
Leave useful toil to howl a dismal lay.

Poor Pegasus! a side-saddle now galls thee;
A woman's aimless hand now sadly hauls thee
From right to left, and to increase thy pains,
She cudgels thy thin flanks and her thick brains.
Let us be just. I doubt not *Lucy Hooper*
Has an o'erflowing mind, when bent to loop her
New over-skirt, or tie her latest bonnet;
But spare, sweet songstress, spare another sonnet!
Immortal Muse! curb, curb thy boundless lay—
Whelm not mankind; oh, crush not helpless clay!
Be not surprised that my appeal thus made is—
The Greeks the Furies called sweet, arch young
        ladies.

All hail, great Mystic! Folly's grand high-priest!
Teacher of moonshine! chief of Error's feast!
Thou wavering *ignis fatuus;* but hist!
E'en now it fades, blent with Oblivion's mist;
While all that follow stumble thro' the fog,
To plunge, at last, deep in some fatal bog.
Behold his page! its sunless waters glide
Currentless—still an ever-ebbing tide;
And lifeless thoughts that here and there may gleam,
Like squeezed-out lemons in a sewer seem—
Sickening the sight; while ghastly objects thud
Against the banks, wrapped in a shroud of mud.

Beneath this veil glides hideous blasphemy,
Scarce merged, to 'scape the scotching preacher's eye.
As in all turbid waters, a slight wreath
Shows where the ugly snake winds on beneath.
Hark! modern Druid—from the night's lone deeps,
Methinks a strange, low, thrilling murmur creeps.
" 'Tis but the rattling of the pine-tree's cone"—
Yet, hark again!—'tis surely louder grown;
A steady throb, as 'twere an army's van—
Yes, yes, a tramp!—hurrah! the Coming Man!
Haste, haste, anticipate thy fate—expire—
Let thy own volumes be thy funeral pyre!—
But when all's o'er and the sad deed is done,
Great Folly'll weep for little *Em, her son.*

"What! say you nothing," some one says, "of *Whit-
        tier?"*
No, nothing—save to wish that he were *wittier.*

Yet one there is, not of this convict crew,
Whose song, tho' timid, weak, and far from new,
And played upon a borrowed reed, is yet
Not void of melody. I would forget
Its faintness—straggling tones are e'en so sweet,
That he alone seems for our praises meet.

What shall I say to thee, thou wretch! that fain
On thy black brow wouldst paint the hue of Cain?
Thou would-be murderess!—if snakes could crawl
To the immortal stars, and make them fall!
Vain, helpless deathling! thou that seek'st for fame
By hurling filth at an eternal name.

Vile harpy! curb thy o'erflowing stomach's flood,
Nor vomit on the great, the wise, the good!
Spectacled ghoul, forbear!—or this my arrow
Shall pierce, if not thy heart, thy festering marrow.
Crawl, viper, crawl! go stow thyself away,
Deep in some hole, far from the light of day.

I've wandered through the silent corridors
And misty vaults of Time, as one explores
The winding catacombs, beginning where
Thick darkness lay around me, and the air
Was close and stifling; but still stumbling on,
I came at last to where a taper shone,
Shedding a feeble, wan, and struggling ray
On many a pictured emblem of decay.
As I passed onward, lights more frequent grew,
Clear-burning sconces floods of radiance threw
O'er sleeping marble forms; while arches wide,
And massy columns rose on either side.
Still farther on such streams of rainbow-light
Lit the vast galleries, that my weak sight
Was dazzled by their splendor; but from here,
Rare and more rare the torches still appear,
Till all once more is dark, where now I stand;
While the dim, flickering rush within my hand
Serves but to awe me and increase the gloom;
No sound disturbs this stillness of the tomb,
Save the faint, constant drip, as on the wall
The water-drops die, one by one, and fall.
Ha! what are these wild forms that here I see
Start from the darkness? Look, they turn on me
Faces all pale with agony. But lo!

The light falls on them, and great portraits glow
Around—immortal sketches! which might well
Seem living forms, so true a tale they tell.
Now closer to the canvas flares the flame—
And under each is written, *Bret Harte's* name.

CANTO SECOND.

Sick of Corruption, Folly, Vice, and Fraud—
Those Protean monsters that now bask abroad,
Like ghastly reptiles daubed with every hue,
Striped, ringed, and spotted, black, and red, and blue,
That from their slimy pool crawl, one by one,
And bake and blister in the noonday sun,
Drawing fresh strength from the envenomed air,
Whose poisoned breath bids all true life despair;
Weary with watching by the State's sick bed,
Seeing the hungry flies swarm round his head,
The strong limbs quivering on convulsion's rack,
The features sharpening and the face grown black;
Heart-sick, and faint, and worn, a strange unrest
Crept thro' my being and my soul oppressed.

With failing hope, I turned toward the Law;
But judges bribed, and juries *packed* I saw,
Both with the culprit pleasantly hobnobbing,
A fellow-feeling in their bosoms throbbing,
Till no man entering there could e'er decide
Which were the triers and which was the tried.
And when a murder new, strange, and laborious
Convulsed the town, 'twas proved most meritorious;
So each strove bravely that he might remove all
Fame from the last, and meet the court's approval.
Then, fearing I should feel the law's full might,
Because I had not risen in the night
To kill my friend, my parents broil or stew,

And had not even burned a town or two—
Oppressed by ultra-civilization's sights,
I moped alone for many days and nights;
Neglecting food, and seldom soothed by sleep,
I shunned mankind, involved in musings deep.

My kindred frowned, as kindred oft will frown;
They said I needed knowledge of the town—
My gloom would quickly vanish should I vie
With young De Poodle in society.
'Tis pity kin are not indeed more rare,
That we might auction them—I see you stare!
But you would sell yours for a single lot
Fronting on Clinton Place.—"But have they not
Our blood within their veins?" Yes, so have gnats,
Fleas, bed-bugs, flies, and sometimes vampire bats.

They've weighed you with all stupid scrupulosity;
Know to a hair your mental ponderosity;
And when on reading, not on trade, you doted,
With kind contempt your life a failure voted.
Flee them as flies the Parthian, with this volley:
The worldling's wisdom is the wise man's folly.
Think not, because each empty day drags o'er,
And leaves their minds just where they were before,
That this indeed is living. Stem the stream,
And be your thought—we are but what we deem.
The lifeless froth lies stranded on the lea,
The wave rolls back and joins its parent sea.
Wouldst thou pluck fruit from shadows on a wall?
Or ocean's coral from a ewer haul?
No: seek not, then, in worldings' souls to find
A single throb for real heart or mind.

Their hearts inclosed in envy's triple steel,
Bid them despise the glow they may not feel;
And telling youth, "No fool but dreams of fame,"
They pass away, and leave no trace or name—
Even as an empty globe of fragile glass
Rolls down a hill, crushing the bright young grass,
And may roll far; but should it chance to meet
The smallest pebble, crashes at your feet.

The age of youth outshadows that of age;
For Feeling dies, ere yet Death's mailed gage
Falls ringing in Life's crumbling court; but when,
In youth, we know our sight shall ne'er again
Meet that which was our all, the bloom still keeps
On Feeling's cheek; yet still the sleeper sleeps:
And though the watchers cry aloud, and tear
Their tresses in the frenzy of despair,
Or chide the passive form with gentlest arts,
The sleeper sleeps—a trance that knows no starts!
The heart may early find its journey o'er,
And wait while partial Death still bars his door;
Too dull for hope, nay, almost for regret—
A darkened dial, whose last sun has set—
A ring within some long lost, moundless grave—
A shell-incrusted anchor 'neath the wave,
Whose bark sank in some unremembered squall—
A sealess beach, a rusted vane, where all
The mighty winds of heaven died long ago,
Which yet doth point whence the last breath did blow.

But I digress from my digressions, which
With their slight wain have but a slender hitch.
Indeed, I hate all method, and but write

My thoughts as they flow on, or dull or bright.
I love this darting, eddy-seeking rhyme,
Since it perchance may 'scape the beak of Time—
That gray crane Time, that wades Life's sombre
    flood,
Seizing bright fish and—leeches 'neath its mud.

Dejected, taunted as unpractical,
I strayed the groves about my father's hall.
It was an ancient mansion, eaveless, low,
With many straggling wings, o'er which the slow,
Untiring vines had clambered, and had hung
Their banners from its butttresses, and clung
Round its wide, sunken windows; the high door
Lay deep within a marble porch, which bore
Two vast white columns, reaching to the roof;
How oft I've hid me here from all aloof,
And crouched beside a pillar, noon beguiled!
Watching with musings known but to a child,
The marble marbled o'er with sleeping beams,
And shadows quivering as some passing dreams
Would break their rest, yet slumbering till the breeze
Should wake them with his whisper to the trees.
Within the spacious grounds tall pine trees stood,
Mixed with the maple, hemlock, buttonwood,
And ashes that towards their bases bent;
Beneath whose boughs, thro' light and shadow, went
Long, winding walks. Of these was one that led
Thro' tangled shrubs, half meeting overhead,
To where 'twas lost, o'ergrown with weeds and grass,
Within a small, dark grove of sassafras,
Whose dusk, o'erhanging arches the bright beams
Of noon made sadder by their struggling gleams.

Beneath there stood, half buried in the gloom,
A broken bench, beside a sunken tomb.

And here in childhood oft alone I've sat
Far in the night, to watch the swerving bat,
And hear the owls from out their chancel dim,
In the dark pines, trill their quaint, quavering hymn;
While tree-frogs with their spirit-voices cried
To unseen clouds to shed their showery tide.
And as the shadows with their noiseless feet,
Now in advance, and now in swift retreat,
In phantom phalanx round me still contended;
And as pale, silver-winged beams descended,
And hovered o'er the youthful upturned face,
Bright with rapt thought and childhood's wild, free
    grace—
Something from out the unseen world there crept
Within my soul, which since has never slept.

And here again, in manhood now I stood,
And watched the sky in sad and musing mood.
The clouds, like troops of mourners veiled and slow,
Wrapped in their dusky cloaks, swept on below
The moon, who thro' their dark and misty ranks
Stole oft a timid gaze; while on the banks
Of the low stream, which crossed the mead beneath,
Tall, shadowy vapors, twisting wreath on wreath,
Wound slowly upwards thro' the distant trees,
Which seemed to wave—and yet I felt no breeze.
Far on the horizon, in a low cloud,
With fitful gleam the summer lightning glowed,
Oft quenched, yet still renewed and glimmering forth,
As if some giant dweller in the North

Snuffed out and lit his candle.—As I gazed,
Still lost in contemplation, half amazed,
I found a strange, wild wish the lonely night
Had breathed into my soul—it was a flight,
Which, leaving this dull world of envious strife,
Should bear me up to heaven, while still in life.

The summer passed; forgotten was my thought,
When suddenly this startling news was brought,
That an old friend — behold what modern pluck
     did!—
After much time and labor, had constructed
A new machine, which did its own inventing,
And made the *thought* of any one that went in
Prepared to pay the owner. Not to waste
So grand a chance, I sought him in all haste.
But trusting not his faith implicitly,
And fearing earthly comrades to the sky,
I asked for something to enable me
To fly up to the top of any tree.
That being wholly given to ornithology,
Science must be this seeming freak's apology.
He ranged some letters, shot a bolt or two,
Twisted a crank, and turned a well-oiled screw;
When swift began a deafening din and clashing,
As if ten thousand giant flails were thrashing;
But soon it ceased, and from an under drawer—
A sort of trough I had not seen before,
He took a pair of ribbed and bat-like wings,
With fastenings for the shoulders—straps and rings.
He bade me try them on. I first obeyed him.
Then wrapped them up, and, as I thanked him, paid
     him.

I hastened home; 'twas dusk. Beside a tree
I stood the wings, then hurried in to tea,
And there, within the circle of the lamp,
My parents' casual chatting shed a damp
Upon my hopes. Why felt they not a thrill?
Why sat they there, so cold, so calm, so still,
While I nerved for the desperate plunge? It seemed
As if they knew I had some plan, but deemed
That any scheme of mine was weak audacity,
And all great deeds beyond my known capacity.
I longed to spring up suddenly, and cry,
"I have bought wings to sail up to the sky.
I told you I'd do something, long ago.
I start to-night! Say, am I aimless now?"
The talk flowed smoothly on, finally turning
On those sweet bourns of youth, where love of learning
Is the only love unknown, and thirst for knowledge is
The only thirst unslaked—American colleges.

I went to college once, but did not stay long;
I could not bear the universal bray, long
Sustained and furious, that around one pours
From lettered dunces and untutored boors.
No place than college is more aristocratic—
A well-bred man is here thought most erratic.
Bright studs, pins, watch-chains, rings on all sides
    gleam;
'Tis as if gentlemen were made by steam—
I do not mean the steam that rises from them—
So bright their feathers are, so ill become them.
Here men with thews of iron, hearts of steel,
Will press your hand until your senses reel;
Your knuckles they from deep affection crush,

But, if you die next day, care not a rush.
Besides, you're soaked in sickening floods of slobber
Rained on you from "November till October,"
By men who worship you for popularity,
But who, if needy, would refuse you charity.
Love is thus rammed, like wadding, down your throat,
And when well-primed, you're touched off, as a vote.
'Tis a sad place, few smiles, still fewer tears—
It proved too much for me before three years.

The meal being o'er, I sought the wings and hid
    them—
Deep in an old and unused drawer I slid them;
Then to the library I hastened, fearing
Suspicion should I long delay appearing.
My father, man of old school taste and breeding,
Ensconced in his wide leathern chair, sat reading
A quaint old book, not much in vogue of late—
"Thoughts on the [apparent] Manners of the Great";
Thoughts on their real ones were less improving.
My mother plied her needle; and unmoving
I leaned upon the mantel, while the blaze
Fell lower in the grate, and a dim haze
Seemed gathering o'er the scene, which faded fast,
As the sad, blended voices of the past
Whispered of all seen, heard, thought since my birth,
Up to the present night—my last on earth.
I started guiltily when some one said
The hour was late, 'twas time to go to bed.

I gained my room, put out the light, and lay
Anxious, and feeling those strange creeps, that day
Still laughs to scorn, and night still brings again,

With that weird little noise, as if a pen
Were scratching on the wainscot; while the ceiling
Gives startling cracks, as it were slowly peeling;
And as we strive to smile, pale hands seem stretched
Around, and every breath, tho' gently fetched,
Sounds strangely loud and ghostly—what a sigh
Of blest relief, should the owl's wild, mournful cry
Break thro' this tingling stillness!

                    When all slept,
Wrapped in my overcoat, I slowly crept
Down the wide stairs as gently as a mouse;
Yet each step shrieked, as it would rouse the house.
I reached the pantry safely, and there made
Three sandwiches, and ate some marmalade.
There being nothing else for tooth-incision,
I in a basket packed my slight provision;
Joining thereto a bottle of strong—soda—
I dared not bring within that blest abode a
Tipple! besides, I could not find the key
Of the wine-room. A moment more I'm free!
I next drew forth my wings from the deep drawer,
Then stopped a moment at the unlocked door.
My friends will drag the river Delaware;
Well, be it so! they will not drag it far;
Down to the sea, at most, or to its source,
Which, now I do bethink me, would be worse.
Ere my soliloquy proceeded more,
I heard a step upon the upper floor;
So fastened on my wings, all firm and tight,
And wandered forth alone into the night.
But still one last farewell I had to take,
For ancient love and dear old friendship's sake;

So towards the kennel turned to drop one tear
O'er my poor bull-dog, ere I left the sphere.
But when, after long groping 'mongst the straw,
I patted his broad head and shook his paw,
Wishing to have a little parting chat,
Bid him not grieve, and mourn me, and all that,
He only licked my hand and gave a yawn;
So leaving him, I walked out on the lawn.

A clear, still winter's night; the moon on high
Pours floods of wavering silver from the sky,
Which glancing thro' the leafless trees, below
Trace curious net-work o'er the crusted snow.
Before me tower the pyramidal pines,
Dark, sombre, solemn, tho' the clear light shines
Around; an awsome, hushing whisper creeps
Thro' their dim tops—a sound which never sleeps,
Sad as the ceaseless murmur of the sea—
A spirit's sigh, borne from Eternity!
Their fringes by this unfelt air are bent,
While the stars twinkle where the storms have rent
Some rift in their dark sails. A hazy glow
Lit the near horizon, where just below
The outskirts of the monster city ran,
Whence came the unvarying, constant hum of man,
Marring still Nature's sleeping harmony.
A cock crew, and his dreary, ghostly cry
Rose strangely mingled with the silence deep,
Weird as the murmur of one lost in sleep;
Still clinging to the air, the dreamy tone
Slow died away, leaving night doubly lone.
I started at the cry, and turning, saw,
With a strange yearning not unmixed with awe,

The dark, old house, with moonlit ivy crowned,
Gaze on its darker shadow, which still frowned
From its cold, captive bed, upon the moon.
I stood and looked farewell, in sad commune
With thoughts, not people, of the past—when lo!
A shutter creaked, and a long, straggling glow
Shot thro' the night. I choked the farewell sigh,
And springing upward, soared into the sky!
Down, down, the earth sank reeling from my gaze;
Moon, stars swam round, blent in one misty blaze;
Sick, dizzy, blind, rushing I knew not where,
Yet undismayed, I madly beat the air.
When sense returned, the great, dark earth was gone,
And in its place a humble planet shone,
While countless mighty orbs above, beneath,
Majestically rolled. I paused for breath,
And gazing down from the bright starlit dome,
I saw, or thought I saw, my childhood's home;
The graceful linden waving at the door,
The yellow waves of sunlight rippling o'er
The arbor where my father sat and read;
My childhood's songs; the faces of the dead;
Youth's dream of fame while gazing on the sea—
The dash of billows heard in infancy.
All these rushed back from the far-wafted years!
Strange tho' it seem, my eyes grew dim with tears.
How strange it is that, leaving things we loathe,
Some vines of memory still the ruins clothe!
We fain would feel rejoiced, yet are not glad;
Even from those we hate, good-by sounds sad.
Words like to these broke from my pensive lips:
"Farewell, slight shallop 'mongst unnumbered ships!

Tossed by Time's changing weather, o'er thy side,
Death's waves are breaking—see, thy seams yawn
    wide!
While wildest passions rack the faces blue
Of thy o'er-crowded, cramped, and shivering crew.
But I am free! Why 'gainst thee, Earth, rebel?
No more I plunge the bucket in Truth's well,
Ten thousand wriggling, crawling lies to raise.
The sting of Censure, and the die of Praise,
The dirk of Envy, and cold Hatred's spear,
I smile at now—each, all are helpless here!
Part we in peace! thy mingled spell is out.
No prisoner leaves his prison with a shout,
But wrings his jailor's hand half tenderly,
And loves the broken chain that proves him free!
I sudden ceased; for two worlds in full view,
Met, crashed in asteroids—the splinters flew
Around—one brushed my knee, one grazed my cap;
I plied my wings to 'scape from more mishap.

Ere long a meteor, darting thro' the sky,
Essayed my new-fledged powers of flight to try.
'Twas a close race—he traveled very fast;
But losing breath, at length was fairly past.
I still swept onward thro' the sky—but hark!
'Tis the fierce Dog-star's constant, savage bark;—
"If my good bull were here, you saucy fellow!
He'd change your barking to a dismal bellow."
But soon my upward progress thro' the air
Was intercepted by the Northern Bear;
He gave a growl, and stretched his paws so wide
That space was none to pass on either side.
Then, thinking that a shot would prove a damper,

I drew the soda-bottle from my hamper
And hurled it at his head. My aim was nice;
But Bruin caught the bottle, in a trice
Popped out the cork, and guzzled down the soda,
Like a hot Englishman in a pagoda.
But this took time, and ere he could recover
I was far, far away—tho' not "in clover."
'Tis true he threw the bottle in my wake,
But as to distance made a vast mistake;
It only hit the Dog-star on the jowl,
Making him dance with pain, and madly howl.

And now the fair *Andromeda* appears,
Bright, blooming, buxom, not at all in tears;
Her lovely, slender figure half displayed,
A flame of love had in an iceberg made.
My heart throbbed—a soft sigh I seemed to hear;
So, ogling her, instinctively drew near.
A meaning smile, a glance, an air alert,
Showed willingness, and even desire to flirt.
But *Perseus* hastening up with great ferocity,
I thought it best to curb my curiosity.
The way he swung the hissing Gorgon's head
Had filled King Richard, or the Cid, with dread.
I whistled loud, to show my unconcern,
But fled away like steam from out an urn.

Orion smiled on me as I sped by—
I caught a twinkle in his northern eye;
But, fearing to appear a parvenu—
A half-cut, shoddy, or a mushroom new,
If breeding or politeness I should show him,
I looked away, pretending not to know him.

Enraged at this, he quickly drew his sword,
And death had here been snobbery's reward;
But as the weapon from its scabbard flew,
And I already felt myself in two,
The Bull "put in" a frantic, furious charge,
Making *Orion* use both sword and targe;
And now began a deadly, fearful fray,
The heavens shook as doth a housewife's tray;
Orion swore, the Bull as loudly bellowed—
But I sped on till space their howlings mellowed.

Fair *Cassiopeia* in her easy-chair
Rocking on her soft Axminster of air,
Just as I settled to a desperate pace,
Gave a slight nod, and called to me thro' space,
Begging I'd come and have some friendly talk—
A lady's whims one may not dare to balk;
So, lounging at her feet, I tried the rule
To prove: *the purer ton, the greater fool.*
Thrice-blest society! I pray, did you
E'en forge this touchstone, pure, unerring, true?
Or came it from Zenocrates, or Plato,
Seneca, Solon, Socrates, or Cato?
"Old Ockham's razor" is a fruit-knife found,
When placed beside this cork-screw of the monde;
This draws a mental bottle in a jiffey,
The aspirant is tested quick, and if he
Has the least taste, he's dashed upon the ground
With, *No wine's fit to drink that's not unsound.*
And then, Society is so exclusive
(Of sense, I mean.)—but this you'll think abusive;
In truth, all this is chiefly spite in me,
Being thrust out long ago for gaucherie:

That is, I dared to think that well-bred tameness
Meant pure stupidity and helpless sameness;
('Tis said that man a paltry ape began—
I think the ape's descended from the man.
They've reached the point to which we're only tend-
 ing—
All thoughts and manners to one model bending:
This is my theory—ere you jeer and scoff it,
Consult with Stuart Mill, our modern prophet.)
So, with an ancestor in each Crusade,
In this, the last, I drew my rusty blade.

T' our tale. The lady plied me with much prattle,
Sad scandal, slander, gossip, tittle-tattle—
How Mars came home quite drunk the other night,
And threw his mistress into such a fright!
Jove's youngest had walked little since her mar-
 riage—
Some hinted she had suffered a miscarriage.
The fair even cast a slur on Pallas' name;
Said she was sadly trifling with her fame;
Wondered that to the point she did not bring *him*,
Or save appearances and seem to fling him.
All this, and more, delayed my upward flight—
I really feared she'd chatter all the night;
When, giving her wide silks a modest rustle,
She asked the exact shape of the latest bustle;
And when I flatly said I did not know,
She tossed her head, and told me I might go.

After long flight, the dawn's faint, greenish hue
Went stealing up thro' the deep midnight blue,
Making the paling stars look wan and faded—

Like some poor beauty, weary, worn, and jaded,
Whom flirting, love, dancing from twelve till five,
Have made seem dead, much rather than alive.
In her see Civilization's dearest child!
Poor thing! so sadly gay, so tamely "wild."
Alas! she's seen so much, and yet so little—
Life's dreariness, the whole—life's joy, no tittle;
For night to her means dancing, day means dining,
The rest is naught, save dressing and repining.
She pines for Nature, which she never saw;
Feeling, she's learned, means being a *cat's paw;*
Wrong means, to her, the censure of a clique,
And right means cheating it with tingeless cheek;
Nature, a well-waxed floor; the sky, a ceiling;
Mankind, a ball-room; love, a coxcomb kneeling;
This is her knowledge, graced with some assump-
    tion—
For her the best thing gained is her consumption;
For soul being dead, the body should be following—
But I'm digressing and I hear you hollowing
To call me back—so e'en must be less serious,
And change my style, since Satire's self may weary
    us.

The stars were gone, chased by the rosy light.
A vast, dark object rose upon my sight;
As I drew near I saw it was a world,
All flat beneath; above white fog-wreaths curled
Volume on volume, rolling swift away,
Borne on the fragrant breath of the young day.
Upon the horizon great mountains rose,
Upon whose lofty peaks the virgin snows
Blushed crimson 'neath the glowing kiss of morn;

Between these and the coast, rough, jagged, torn
And rocky, lay a broad and rolling vale,
Whence such sweet fragrance floated on the gale,
So pure, so bland, so redolent of peace,
I knew 'twas heaven, and glad my flight to cease,
I closed my wings, and lighted on the shore—
Earth's toil was past, Earth's ceaseless turmoil o'er.

Here, reader, let us pause and rest awhile,
Even as a traveler perches on a stile.
I hear you cry aloud, "We've journeyed far,
And had some fighting, but no open war."
Have patience, and within the coming canto
We'll try to win o'er Vice a new Lepanto.

Lest vulture critics on this satire pounce,
And tear the poor, weak thing, I here announce
That poetry, not satire, my true trade is—
I mean to write an Epic for the ladies:
In seven cantos shall the poem be,
Each one as lengthy as my present three.
The first shall be of babies, with some hints
On bird-eye, teething, vomiting, and squints:
My next shall treat of trimming, flouncing, skirting;
The third will be an episode on flirting;
The fourth and fifth shall both be imitations
Of Homer's catalogue of ships and nations,
And carefully detail, tho' this seems few,
Some fifteen thousand of engagements new;
And in the sixth, unless by death I'm hindered,
I'll give the mischief-makings of their kindred;
But, that complaint may have not even a handle,
The seventh and last shall touch on naught but
    Scandal.

CANTO THIRD.

The sun peeped o'er the mountain tops, and threw
Long shadows, which went stalking o'er the dew
That sprinkled all the valley. Soon his beams
Fell glittering on a thousand lakes and streams,
And at my feet in rainbow sparkles flashed
O'er a quick, loud cascade, that madly dashed
From rock to rock, with many a splash and hiss,
Plunging in space, lost in the vast abyss.
I climbed the rocks, wet with the falling spray,
And gained the border of a mead which lay
Between the coast and woodlands on the right,
From which the stream came winding into sight.
Here, sitting on a mossy stone, I ate
A sandwich, with a plaintain for a plate.
But I was weary, and the sun on high
Began to hurl down lava from the sky;
I hurried o'er the mead, reached a deep grove
And, needing rest, ere I could farther rove,
I sat me down, reclined against a tree,
And ate two sandwiches—which makes my three.

'Twas a sweet spot: the stream went rippling by,
Singing the song of solitude; the sky
Seemed pillowed in its depths; a fleecy cloud,
Within whose snowy folds the sunlight glowed,
Stole on athwart its mirror; while a breeze,
Softer than that above, stirred in the trees
That grew beneath its surface. But below,

Like flights of arrows from a fairy bow,
Their wavering way the glancing sunbeams took
Down thro' the moving waters of the brook;
And as the leaves above stirred, wandering ranks
Of shadows to and fro upon the banks
Strayed drowsily; my head drooped, languor crept
With noiseless step upon me, and I slept.

When I awoke the scene was changed; the sun
Was sinking in the west, the clouds were dun;
The trees' long shadows thro' the failing light,
To join and welcome in their parent night,
Crept eastward. Fearing darkness ere I could
Gain some abode, I hurried thro' the wood;
O'er fallen logs, and brush, and vines I strode—
The glade was narrow—soon I reached a road,
A turnpike broad which skirted round the wood.
But here in some perplexity I stood,
Uncertain whether it were best to turn
To right or left; so plucked a bit of fern
And tossed it up—towards the right it flew—
I hastened on, deeming the omen true.

I found the sun was higher than I thought,
An hour of day remained; my pace soon brought
Me to a sign-board, where I learned the town
Was only two miles distant. Care was thrown
By this from off my mind, and soon I reached
A gentle hill, whence the wide valley stretched
Before me; and from here I could descry
Thick smoke and blazing chimneys 'gainst the sky.
Then strange misgivings o'er me 'gan to creep—
When lo! a coach and six dashed up the steep;

In it an aged man came swiftly riding—
A moment more, I knew the poet Dryden.
Seeing me standing there, so worn and tired,
He took me in, and turning back, inquired
How I had come from Earth, and what my pelf;
But, like most talkers, answered all himself;
And as we rode along towards the city,
Chatted delightfully, now grave, now witty.
He said a tube pneumatic had given birth
To wondrous changes, for that pipe from Earth
Had papers brought, and books with new opinions,
Which revolutionized the king's dominions;
The times were changed; the palm was gone, and lyre;
Provisions since were high, and wages higher.
'Twas clear he thought that purposes of trade
Had urged my toilsome journey, for he said:
"You've doubtless seen a rainbow, and have thought it
Extremely pretty—would have gladly bought it,
To dye your zephyrs, or, if such your trade is,
For flounces for the evening silks of ladies;
Or retailed by the yard, to trim a bonnet.
But little deems the man who looks upon it
That it to Heaven leads—a mighty causeway.
Nay, start not; 'tis a misty, magic gauze-way,
Which, tho' vast, inert masses it will bear,
'Neath human feet would melt to empty air."

But here I chanced to get a word between,
And asked him if he took a magazine;
"But one comes here—*Scribner's,* I think you call it—
Hydraulic engines up the causeway haul it.
At druggist's shops alone it can be found;
Its vast weight makes it dear—a cent a pound;

But, being of a potent inky juice full,
In minute doses 'tis extremely useful;
For, if an angel chance a wing to bruise,
Or break an arm, and must the member lose,
'Tis used by us instead of chloroform—
It stupefies them more, and does less harm."

Thus chatting on, we reached the suburbs, where
Great piles of garbage towered in the air,
As if Decay to Filth a monument
Would raise; but farther on, our course was bent
Thro' noble avenues with pavements wide,
While palaces rose high on either side.
But, passing these, the coach drew up before
A quaint, old gabled house, with stepless door.
Seeing my face some wonderment displayed,
In answer to my look the poet said:
"This house alone possesses a firm wall;
The rest, by contract built, are apt to fall."

The poet said next morning: "As a resident,
'Tis right you be presented to the *President.*"
Now, as I thought in Heaven there was no drinking,
I started up and stared full at him, thinking
That he was mad; and should have stared till now.
But, snatching up his hat, he said: "We'll go."
I say I thought they did not drink in Heaven.
But this belief substantial soon was driven
To dwell afar, 'mongst empty hopes and wishes,
That darkly grope about like eyeless fishes;
(Our petty life's a Mammoth Cave, and we
But wishes to get out, and sunlight see,
And some do paddle stronger and swim out,

But find it hard to drop the stone, or gout,
The acid stomach, or the aching heart—
The blind eyes of the soul,—life's chiefest part!)
For in the streets our way we had to thread
Thro' gangs of drunken *loafers*—Dryden said:
"These are the fruit of manufactories,
Tho' most of them are not their employees;
These sally forth, like errant knights of old—
Tho' not like them, alone,—nor like them, bold;
Each bent, by filth to prove himself a true man,
Or grog, or theft, or insult to a woman;
A little grape-shot, interspersed with canister,
Would help them bravely over Hell's low banister.

We gained the Hall; high Heaven's Chieftain sat
Placidly smoking, in a chair of state—
A groaning virtue writhed beneath each castor,—
But still he smoked, not even a puff the faster.
As I approached he rolled his chewed segar,
And asked me if I'd heard about his war.
I, puzzled, sick at heart, but not out-done,
Asked, with an air *dégagé,* for his son;
But Dryden nudged me in the ribs, and said,
I'd better say but little on that head,
The boy was in the army—with a salaam,
I passed along, feeling not unlike Balaam.

We turned to view the Senate chamber, where
The State's celestial delegates repair.
If e'er you've been in Venice, you remember
That stepping from the train, the engine's ember
Fell red and hissing in the moonlight wave
Of the dark Adriatic, and you gave

A hurried glance, and stepped into a boat,—
And found yourself, you scarce knew how—afloat.
So here we reached the vestibule, when lo!
We stood upon a quay, and just below
There rolled a yellow tide, that swashed and splashed
Against its marble wharf—sudden there dashed
Some spray across my face that twang, that smack
    —oh,
Disgusting thought! it is—it is tobacco!
Ere I had quelled the quick, rebellious stomach,
I saw a gondolier thro' filth and scum make
His way to us. He pointed to his bark—
We entered, and wound on thro' long and dark
Canals and passages; while on our ears
There came strange sounds of distant groans and
    cheers,
As of a far-off conflict, but still soft,
Quenched by the winding walls, oft raised, and oft
Sunk to a whisper, mingled with the splash,
As fell our oar with intermittent plash.
Sudden we turned an angle of the wall—
A deafening roar—we shot into the Hall.
Here lay a broad dark flood, with many isles,—
Senators at their desks, reared high on piles.
Moored to each seat a bark lay gently knocking
Against the posts, and with each wavelet rocking.
Just as we entered, some one loudly cried:
"The gentleman upon the left has lied"—
The speaker yelled: "There should be no debate.
The vote is on this last remaining State,
Which, like the rest, belongs to me and you,
For service rendered, and for *back pay* due."
'Twas voted.—On a platform at his side,

Their trade unhallowed hosts of jugglers plied;
Strange robes they wore, high caps, and gilded collars,
And swallowed long strings,—not of pearls,—but
    dollars;
And bowing low, adown their cavernous throats
Crammed mass on mass, whole handfuls of bank-
    notes:
But, unlike other jugglers I have seen,
Nothing came out of all that they put in.
Methought the senators had been well used
To this display, they seem not even amused;
Some laughed, some slept, some on their desks carved
    lizards—
Some said the jugglers should be hung, as wizards.

Reader, since I have tried to prove of late,
That if not well, at least I could relate,
I'll now describe, without narration's cooings,
Tell what I saw, and dock my private doings.

Beside the eastern gate, within a park,
There stands a row of buildings long and dark!
The whole a satire upon architecture,
So well planned, that where'er you may direct your
Astonished gaze, it meets some low burlesque
Upon Corinthian, Gothic, arabesque,
Much Babylonian too, Ionic, Doric—
With native styles that ape the pre-historic;
Above, below, each space completely filled in
With strange conglomerate filth, that natural gilding.
"What means this mass in Heaven," I asked of Dry-
    den,
"Which only Satan's self could take a pride in?"

He answered: "This is the abode of knowledge—
The synonym on earth, you know, 's a college."
The spacious portal frowned above my head,
And gazing upward, I this motto read,
Emblazoned o'er the gate in red and yellow—
"Worth makes the man, and want of it the *fellow*."

Beyond this gate there stands a lofty door
Of massive oak, and quaintly studded o'er
With brazen nails and brightly burnished knobs—
Here enter boors, to come out fops and snobs.
Just as upon a sign-board I have seen
A cunningly constructed, vast machine,
Where filthy pigs, and dogs, pell-mell they threw
Into one end, and from the other flew
Hair-brushes, gloves,—pomade, a perfect sluice
    full—
True, nothing else—'twas curious, if not useful.
Enter with me by that low wicket there,
Turn to the right, now up that trembling stair.
See you this vault, that rotting desk that leans
Towards those benches!—here are daily scenes
That would draw floods from Caracalla's eyes,—
Yet pause with me, I would apostrophize.

Immortal Homer! hadst thou ever known,
What man may never know, the fate thine own,
That not a blessing, but a curse, should be
Thy deathless fame and immortality,—
On Chian shore, thy harp thou ne'er hadst strung,
But in the sea the tuneful bauble flung!
Kind reader, shed, for gentle Pity's sake,
A sorrowing tear o'er him whose lyre could wake

The echoes of Eternity: for Death
Here conquers immortality, and breath
Deserts th' undying one, each day he dies,
Yet ever lives—an endless sacrifice.
Behold e'en now the blind old bard is led
Forth to his torture; round his sacred head
How green the wreath that yields no leaf to Time!
What glory lights that sightless face sublime!
"Come, brains of oak!" the master cries, "come,
    rally!"
"On Thought and Feeling one more gallant sally!
Our ancient words of courage, Texts and Rules!
Down, down with sense! St. Dunstan, and close
    fools!"
And first some pelt the bard behind, before,
With oaken blocks from their own heads, and ore
Drawn from that great lead mine, the master's
    brain,—
Let me curtail this sickening theme of pain,—
Would truth permit, I'd gladly end it here—
A rotten egg now greets him in the ear,
And as he turns, an ill directed boulder,
From the Professor's cranium breaks his shoulder,—
The next, aimed better, crushes in his head,—
And god-like Homer, prince of bards, is dead.

Beyond lie other vaults, where neophytes
Are daily exercised in sacred rites,
Appointed by their great god Ignorance,
To keep their minds in constant, due defense,
Lest his arch adversary, Meaning, should
Invade their ranks in some unguarded mood.
Above are dormitories, cell-like, drear—

What need I more? all's dull and heavy here.
Even their mirrors are unwieldy tools;
The teachers donkeys use—the scholars mules.
"Are not their brains kicked out?" I hear you cry.
Never—yet seek not, reader to know why;
This is a solemn mystery. God wot,
I would divulge no secrets—let us not
Probe theirs; yet this, to prove that I have been
Fair to both sides, without a tinge of spleen—
If taught and tutors should their seats reverse,
'Twould be no better, and, I fear, no worse.

Close to the city lies a low morass,
And in its midst a pond, where scum, and grass,
And loathely slime, on the black waters float;
A club has bought this spot, and here devote
Their days to mirth—they sport them in the slime,
And growing black, obscurity begrime.
Passing the place, we climbed an eminence,
Whence we might overlook their lofty fence.
Without, there foamed a filthy ink-stained crowd,
Tattered in garb, with voices harsh and loud,
Looking as if they lived on scarce a pittance,
Wildly, yet vainly, striving for admittance.
These, hustling, jostling, jamming, crushing, swear-
    ing,
Were, by their very violence, impairing
Their chance to pass the gate, for here most stuck,
Mashing each other into nameless muck.
I mean the outer gate, for, just beyond,
A latticed wicket sacred held the pond.
But here there stood a solemn, grand Inquisitor,
To catechize each fresh-arriving visitor,

And try his mind—if gold, or lead, or tin—
That only perfect dunces might pass in.
For all that had a single grain of sense
They quickly seized and threw them o'er the fence;
Here falling far, they gained no little dirt,
And thought themselves, sometimes, a good deal hurt.
Now from this dismal club our steps we bent;
But I asked Dryden, ere we farther went,
What it was called, and purely at a venture, he
Said he believed the name it bore was *Century*.

As lurks the bee within the blooming flower,
So danger waits us in each reckless hour.
Full in our path a hideous monster stood,
Glaring around as if in search of food.
An ass's head it bore, while to and fro
Its ears flapped strangely, with a motion slow;
A goose's neck this to the body joined;
A reptile's trunk it had, and far behind
A monkey's tail hung pendulous; it flew
With owlet's wings, and talons had it too:
Formed to strike terror to all human hearts,
A sickening mixture of conglomerate parts,
Strangely assorted, and together packed ill—
In short, a sort of sacred *Pterodactyl*.
At sight of me it gave a horrid bray,
But, seeing Dryden, shrieked and fled away.
As I had drawn a pistol, fearing harm,
The poet bade me lay aside alarm;
He said the brute the name of *Critic* bore,
And he had hurt it badly years before.

Far from the city, visited by few,
Remote and desolate, a glade of yew
And cypress stands in a dim, lonely vale;
And here, while o'er their heads the fitful gale
Waves the dark mourners' plumes, all sad and slow,
The poets of the past stray to and fro.
With downcast mien they wander ever on,
Their laurels blanched, neglected, and alone.
Sad Pilgrims of the soul!—lone travelers! they
Who, as they passed, fired beacons on life's way,
To light us to Eternity; tho' we
Dare follow not, and few their radiance see.
Here have I loitered oft to muse and jest
With one, at times, less mournful than the rest
(Whose dauntless Muse may smile at change and
        time,
Varied as Nature is, nor less sublime),
In pilgrim garb,—no more with Greek attire on—
His name the synonym for greatness—Byron.
Talking of poetry one day, he said,
That when he lay in Missolonghi, dead,
Trelawney in his search had failed to find
One paper that he thought had slipped behind
The bureau; and he then repeated me
Some stanzas, which he said he meant should be
Inserted in *Don Juan,* near the end
Of the first canto, when he next should send
To England, answering to a petition
From Murray to augment the next edition.
I now can only three of them recall,
Tho' there were, as I think, some ten in all.

I.

'Tis sweet at even, from the lonely strand
To watch the sunset glow spread o'er the sea
Its rosy splendor; it is sweet to stand
Beside some forest brook, whose bubbling glee,
In mirthful dashings, or in murmurs bland,
Pours music on the ear; and sweet to me
Are the bright fancies, which at twilight's hour
Shed o'er the heart the fullness of their power.

II.

'Tis sweet, returning from far lands, to view
That spot we call our home; 'tis sweet to hear
A lovely woman say she loves but you—
That you of all men are to her most dear;
'Tis doubly sweet to think her words are true.
(You're lucky if her flame survive the year!)
But oh, young men! to you my best advice is,
All women hold their love at too high prices.

III.

One asks your love, another asks your money—
Both pleasant things to have, but hard to give;
Deep, fervid love gains little of life's honey,
And love in shackles will not deign to live.
What kind's the best, then, since we must have one? I
Think all resemble water in a sieve;
But when a lady talks of being proper,
I yawn aloud, take up a book, and—drop her.

There is a mighty company, that fain
Would build a monstrous dome, to stop the rain
Of small commodities, that frequent falls
From other stars; the vast, half-circling walls
Have passed the clouds, yet they would build them
     higher,
Till they have forced each one to be a buyer
Of their own goods. But they will ne'er succeed;
Or, should they so, ruin will be their meed,
For their vast dome must bar heat, sunlight, air,
And leave them naught save darkness and despair.

'Twas early night; the air was clear and still.
I stood and gazed from a low, grassy hill,
Where, far as eye might pierce to North and East,
Ruins on ruins stretched—Destruction's feast!
But I was told that man, not Time, had made
These mighty ruins; that the pick and spade,
Not scythe, had caused this havoc; for I learned
That these were mills by their own workmen burned,
Because the owner was of means bereft
To satisfy their cravings; but, when left
With naught to do, they sent a deputation
To bid him make most instant preparation
To build them up—but here they put their *leg* in:
After some search, they found the owner begging
From house to house; then, amply to requite him
For this bad course, and thoroughly to spite him,
They sought their homes and starved themselves to
     death—
Cursing the man they wrecked, with their last breath.
But now bats flit around, and the owl screams
His dismal hootings; while the moonlight streams

With a wan lustre o'er the roofless walls,
And here and there a pale beam glittering falls
On some vast engine's shaft, half merged in clay—
I shuddered at the sight, and turned away.

High on a lofty crag, a mighty fane
Lifts its dark mass above the city's plain;
Domes, columns, arches, battlements, and towers,
Raised pile on pile by the Titanic powers
Of files of ages—forming a strange whole,
So vast, so measureless, the gazer's soul
Reels back, awed, crushed, bewildered. O'er its walls,
Thro' a rent cloud, the slanting sunlight falls,
Glowing o'er sculptures, carvings, bas-reliefs,
Depicting human sufferings, woes, and griefs.
All-potent Crime, sole goddess of the State,
Is worshiped here alike by small and great.
I pass the portal. In the midst, on high
The goddess sits, while round her constantly
A hundred censers cloudy fumes exhale,
Shrouding her form in a thick, smoky veil;
But, rising o'er the mist, defined and clear,
Two faces joined and Janus-like appear.
One bears a forced, insinuating smile
On its lank visage, striving to beguile;
No confidence it wins, but, in its stead,
That deadly, placid look wakes wildest dread;
For wandering movements change the features thin,
As wicked thoughts were crawling 'neath the skin.
Watched by the half-closed, snaky eyes, behold
An altar, blazoned o'er with cloth of gold,
By the vast weight of countless gifts oppressed.
But four are greatly prized above the rest:

Lowest in rank, a *lawyer's brief* is seen
Just peeping from its modest bag of green;
But higher, raised upon the next division,
In full view lies a *Congressman's commission;*
Basking forever 'neath the dreadful smile,
A *railway's charter* crowns the lofty pile;
Highest of all, the altar's very binnacle,
A *ballot-box* gleams on the topmost pinnacle;
And on a flag drooped from a golden rod,
The emblem of the whole is written—*"Fraud."*
The other face—that awful face! a chill
E'en now creeps thro' my veins, despite my will.
'Tis a pale face—so pale 'tis almost blue;
And damp it looks, as sprinkled with Death's dew.
The rolling eyes will on a sudden fix,
The features stiffen, and then wildly mix
Into one mad convulsion; while there drips
A bloody foam from the torn, twitching lips.
And when the eyes thus fix, and still seem glazing,
Following their motion you behold them gazing
Upon a high, black altar, built in tiers,
Where at its top a crimson word appears—
That word is *"Murder."* Just above there swings
An ever-burning, flaring lamp, that flings
A glow o'er various offerings at the shrine.
But four there are pre-eminent, divine:
Lowest and least a guillotine there stands,
Reeking with gore and smoking heads and hands;
Still higher up a *mitrailleuse* is placed,
With all its deadly ammunition graced;
Close to the top, beneath the glassy eyes,
In state a *doctor's full diploma lies;*
Above them all, touching the crimson name,

A small black volume stands, within a frame,
And, gilded o'er its cover dark and polished,
"Capital punishment should be abolished."

To these twin shrines there streams a blended throng
Of motley pilgrims: some weak, others strong;
Some young, some old—with *cloaks* of every hue;
Some bearing olive-wands, some sprigs of yew;
Some gay, and others stern and deathly pale.
And staggering some, with faces flushed and hale,
And blood-shot eyes, and garlands of the vine—
But these all bend their steps to *Murder's* shrine.

Twilight is fallen—hark! the temple-bell!
Thro' the long night its deep tones sink and swell,
Borne on the wind; now faint, now loud, it guides
To Crime's vast fane the ceaseless pilgrim tides.

———————

I stand upon high Heaven's extremest verge—
A rocky cliff, whose base the aërial surge
Washes forever; twilight closes round,
While the far landscape in a sleep profound
Is hushed; a single spire against the sky
Bespeaks the distant city. Here have I,
Reader of earth, penned this strange tale to thee;
For, gazing down thro' awful space, I see,
Faintest in ray, and deepest far below,
A starlet, shedding a faint, ruddy glow.
They say it is the world, and that its beam
Is thus ensanguined by blood's ceaseless stream.
If e'er in this my rhyme on earth I've seemed,
'Twas that in thought I oft myself have deemed

Amongst my kind; that my o'er flowing heart
Has kindled with my lay, till I a part
Became of what I sung. One change I'll ring,
And then from this high rock the poem fling.
('Twill soon reach earth, tho' all space intervene—
I've ballasted with *Scribner's Magazine*.)
And then to Neptune I will take my flight—
A quiet planet, merged in partial night,
Which, hurled afar by the sun's youthful brawn,
Has little heat to breed Corruption's spawn.

I see the stars like stately ships glide by,
Their port no haven but Eternity!
Vast constellations rise athwart the main,
And rolling on, sink but to rise again.
Here Immortality, with smile sublime,
Looks down on man, the changing child of Time!
But I have shed, tho' far from mortal strife,
Full many an angry tear o'er human life.
And what is life? a half-formed pensive thought,
Uncertain, intricate, with doubtings fraught.
Bewildered still, we hear a stranger's tread,
And, starting with a shudder, lose the thread—
A strange inscription on a desert-stone,
O'er which the wind the whirling dust has blown,
Ere we to glean its mystic sense allowed;
And man even, as the shadow of a cloud
Whose substance is but vapor—a dim blot
Blown o'er a landscape, without resting-spot.
Despair not! tho' we stumble thro' the night,
A faint streak tells the Future's dawning light.
Tho' man with fogs of crime the earth may mar,
He cannot dim the radiance of one star,

Nor quell the cheering shout of the wild sea—
Triumphant pæan of Eternity!
My leaf e'en now by the night wind is stirred;
The shadows lengthen—blend—my page is blurred.

Reader, farewell! My falt'ring song is sung;
Yet, if the broken notes which I have flung
O'er the wide sea, thou on the beach shouldst hear,
Pray stop a moment, and incline thine ear
To catch their fitful music. Even now
The last string vibrates, and its tone dies low—
Perchance to be forgotten.—Once again,
Farewell! scorn not this strangely mingled strain.